# TRACK OF THE
# POACHER

# Track of the Poacher

## By

## William Wasserman

ISBN 0-9718907-2-2

Cover by Timothy Flanigan

## ALSO BY WILLIAM WASSERMAN

*Wildlife Guardian*

*Game Warden*

*Poacher Wars*

*Trapping Secrets*

*Pennsylvania Wildlife Tails*

*More Pennsylvania Wildlife Tails*

For Andy

Rest in peace, my friend …

VIII

# Introduction

I spent more than half my life tracking down and arresting wildlife poachers from the big city streets of Philadelphia to the rugged mountains of northern Pennsylvania where I pursued them on foot and by vehicle and boat. Along the way, I investigated thousands of game law violations and arrested many career poachers.

My patrol district comprised roughly four hundred square miles where I encountered some of the most unpredictable—and interesting characters under the sun. Some were sort of likable—others, absolutely despicable, but they all had one thing in common: a blatant disregard for our natural resource laws and a sense of fair play.

The incidents recounted in this book are real; however, the stories are based on my memories over a period of years and may differ from the memories of others. I admit to taking some creative liberties with events and to re-creating some of the dialog. I have also given the poachers and their associates fictitious names and have altered their physical descriptions. Any resemblance to actual persons, living or dead, is entirely coincidental.

*If all men were just, there would be no need of valor.*
— Agesilaus

# A Question of Proof

THE TWO MEN STOOD RIGIDLY, their faces frozen with alarm as the deputy strode toward them through the open woods. He was in full uniform, the badge on his green jacket and state emblem on his hat unmistakable in the brilliant morning sun. The men, dressed in camos, had just finished gutting a ten-point buck, antlers heavy and wide. A once-in-a-lifetime trophy reckoned the deputy as he drew near.

He'd visited the same property twenty-four hours earlier. A neighbor had called, upset about the illegal bait he found there. The practice had been going on for years, he complained, which prompted the deputy to ask why it had taken him so long to call. He was told that the property owner had been his friend but they'd had a falling out.

Exact words: "a falling out."

Apparently, it was time for a little payback.

He'd been directed to a wood-framed cabin located along an isolated road that cut through the rugged mountains of northern Wyoming County. Only a handful of locals lived here year round. Nothing went unnoticed. And so Deputy Jeff Pierce wasn't surprised when he walked into a field behind the cabin and found apples, shelled corn, and several salt blocks spread about. The surrounding terrain trampled heavily with deer tracks.

Now, a little more than a football field's length from the bait, he'd come across two hunters as they knelt by a deer in the woods. They stood slowly, blinking in stupefied amazement as he approached: one fat, the other thin, both

13

equally stunned by his presence. With his eyes fixed steadily on the men, Pierce unsnapped his portable radio from his belt and raised it to his face. "Got them."

I was close by on foot. "Ten four," I answered, and started walking in his direction.

Pierce continued another twenty yards until he was face-to-face with the men. "State game warden," he said. "Who killed the deer?"

"I did," said the fat man, his hands streaked with blood. The deer's snow-white underbelly had been sliced wide open, its entrails spilled upon the ground in a loose pile. A large hunting knife lay by its side, its blade thick with gore.

"What's your name?" said Pierce.

"Salvatore," answered the fat man, beaming with pride. "Salvatore Giovanni Vastolano." He was well tanned with dark, smiling eyes and a strong Roman nose. His hair, thick and shining black, was combed straight back over his broad forehead. "Please," he insisted, "call me Sal, save yourself a mouthful." He swept a thick hand toward the open woods encompassing them. "This is my land, and you are most welcome here, officer." Tilting his head toward the other man, he said, "This is my good friend, Nando. Nando, please welcome the gentleman. I'm sure he only came here to congratulate me on my fine kill."

Nando was the physical contradiction of his friend: lean and wiry with a crooked nose and tiny balding head. His frightened eyes darted nervously from the deer back to the deputy. "Morning, officer," he said in a thin voice. "Is there a problem?"

Pierce ignored the question and focused on Sal. "Where's your gun?"

"Gun? Oh no. I got this one the hard way—with a crossbow! Anybody can kill a deer with a gun. It takes real skill to use a crossbow. One shot, too! I left it at my camp when we came back to get the deer."

"Crossbow?" questioned Pierce.

Sal barked a nervous chuckle. "Don't worry, I got a permit! Got a bum shoulder. Can't draw a compound bow anymore—can't drag a deer by myself, either. That's why I asked Nando to help me get this monster out of the woods." He dug a wallet from his back pocket and extracted a state permit for his crossbow.

Pierce took it from him and looked it over. "Who put all the food out behind your camp?"

"I did," said Sal. "I run a guide service for hunters. Put the food out to grow big antlers. Been doing it for ten years."

Pierce glanced down at the buck. "Looks like it's working."

Sal offered a proud smile. "Gotta be close to two hundred pounds, don't you think?"

Pierce raised an eyebrow at Sal. "I think it's gotta be illegal. You're only a hundred yards from the bait at your camp."

"Whoa!" yelped Sal. "I didn't shoot it here, if that's what you're thinking. I shot the deer way back at my treestand. This is where he dropped—where I found him, that's all."

Pierce heard my footsteps in the dry leaves behind him. He glanced over his shoulder and signaled me forward with a wave. "Wasserman is coming," he told the men. "Let's see what he has to say."

After collecting hunting licenses and IDs from the suspects, I knelt by the buck to examine it. There was a single entrance wound behind the right shoulder, the crisscrossed incision indicating the deer had been struck with a broadhead arrow, or bolt as they're called when fashioned for crossbows. I took my folding knife and cut a small patch of hide from around the incision to expose the pink muscle underneath. The razor-sharp broadhead had sliced neatly through the deer's flesh, driving the bolt between its ribs and into the chest cavity. I grabbed a leg and flipped the carcass

15

over. There was an exit wound showing that the deadly missile had passed through the carcass in a straight line.

I glanced up at Sal. "Where were you when you shot this deer?"

"Back at my treestand, just like I told your deputy."

"Can't be," I said. "Your deer was shot straight through. The bolt didn't come from above."

"Yeah, exactly," agreed Sal. "That's because I was standing at the foot of the tree. Never said I was up in the treestand. I'm too old and too fat to climb anymore."

One look at Sal and you had to believe him. No way he could climb a makeshift ladder into a treestand. I placed the tip of my knife into the deer's paunch, unzipping the gray and bulging organ from end to end. It popped like a lanced boil, a yellow pasty substance of partially digested corn and apples spilling over its sides and oozing to the ground.

Sal and Nando exchanged glances of apprehension as I wiped my blade on the deer's hide. I stood and pocketed the knife. Looking at Sal, I said, "I'd like to see your treestand."

"Sure thing, warden," he said. "But it's a long ways from here."

"I've got plenty of time."

Sal grinned and offered a passive shrug. "Of course. The deer will keep. Come!" He motioned for me to follow and started walking north into the woods.

I shadowed him while Deputy Pierce stood by with Nando. Even if I found evidence that the buck was shot back at his treestand, I still planned to arrest Sal. The fact that its stomach was crammed with the same stuff he'd put behind his cabin was verification that it had been feeding on the bait. We were in the middle of a deep forest, there were no apple trees or cornfields anywhere near us.

The air was brisk and cool under a blue sky, the sun warm on my face as we made our way to the treestand. Typical for Pennsylvania's north woods, any vegetation that had sprouted over the summer had been promptly gobbled up by the tremendous deer herd. Even though we were on level ground with travel relatively easy in the open woods, Sal, who was in his late fifties with a great protruding belly, huffed and puffed while plodding along in a clumsy, hobbling gait.

I could have run five miles in the time it took us to reach his treestand. Sal had to stop and catch his breath every hundred yards or so, and I couldn't help but wonder how long it would be before his clock stopped ticking.

The treestand, a four-foot-square platform of heavy wooden planks fifteen feet above the ground, had been built amid the sturdy branches of a giant oak. The only way up was by a crude ladder of wooden boards nailed to the tree. He turned to me and pointed, his thick brow glistening with sweat. "There it is, warden," he breathed. "Like I say, it's a long way from my cabin."

It was obvious that the treestand hadn't been used in years. Its base was littered with dead branches and decaying leaves, and two of the wooden rungs had fallen to the ground, making a climb to the top all but impossible. Sal walked over to the tree, leaned his back against its broad trunk, and eased his heavy frame to the ground.

"Whew!" he puffed. "I need to rest a moment."

I walked in a graduated circle around the tree looking for bait, continuing to range farther and farther with each rotation until I could no longer see the treestand. There was nothing. No surprise, really. Sal had been so eager to take me here that I didn't expect to find anything. Still, I wanted to squeeze him a little, see how many lies I could catch him in.

I walked back to Sal. He'd fallen asleep at the oak, head cocked back against its thick bark, mouth wide open as he snored and snorted. He was loud—loud enough to scare off half the deer in the county, I reckoned. His jacket lay in a heap on the ground next to him. He wore only a white T-shirt, a ring of dark sweat encircling his open neck. I tapped the sole of his boot with my toe. His eyes flicked open in surprise. "Huh?"

"Show me where the deer was standing when you shot it."

Sal wiped a trickle of drool from the corner of his mouth with a sleeve and eyed me cautiously. "Why do you need to know that?"

"Thought I might find some blood or scuffmarks—proof to corroborate your story."

"I can't do that."

"Can't—or won't?"

Sal dropped his gaze and began to study his boots in silence. His refusal to cooperate confirming that he hadn't shot a deer near his treestand. There was no need to coax him for an explanation.

"Let's head back and take a look behind your cabin," I said.

Sal reached for his jacket with a groan of exertion and struggled to his feet. Then he leaned back against the oak and looked at me. "Sure, we can do that. But I already told your deputy that I put the apples and corn back there. I got nothing to hide."

"To lure deer?"

"That's right. And we got some dandy bucks running around here as a result." He threw his jacket over a shoulder and gave me a toothy smile. "When we get to the cabin I'll have breakfast for us. I'm starved! Walking always kindles my appetite. You must be hungry too."

"Breakfast?" I questioned, thinking I'd misheard.

"Of course! You are my guest! Please! Celebrate my good fortune with me. Nando is a fabulous cook!"

He saw my puzzled look, my unwillingness to accept, and before I could refuse his offer, he let out a wild howl of laughter. "What? You think I keep Nando around only to help me drag my kills? Ha! You are mistaken! How about some nice Italian sausage smothered in peppers and onions—a little pineapple sprinkled in. It's to die for, my friend!"

*Friend?* I couldn't help but wonder if he had any idea how much trouble he was in.

"Come! Eat with me," he beckoned. Then he turned and started plodding through the woods.

I stood watching for a moment, baffled by his good-natured manner.

"Hope I'm not moving too fast for you," he called over his shoulder. There was a smile in his voice.

We stopped back at the kill site before heading to Sal's place. Evidence photos would be crucial if the case went to court. I took a small digital camera from my coat pocket and snapped a dozen photographs of the buck, zeroing in on the entrance wound in its chest before taking some close-up shots of its cleaved paunch. When I was satisfied that I had enough photos, I picked a pencil-sized stick off the ground and pushed the tip into the buck's partially digested stomach contents. I scooped up a dollop of the pulpy goo, shook it into a plastic evidence bag, and zipped it tight. Although I knew it was partially digested bait from Sal's camp, I wanted to be sure that I had a sample for the State Police Crime Lab in case I needed to have it analyzed for a court trial.

When my deputy and I started dragging the deer away, it became clear to Sal and Nando that their trophy buck was going to be confiscated. They said nothing, however, and followed us in silence as we hauled the heavy carcass a hundred yards over broken terrain to their camp.

When we finally cleared the woods, we broke into a stretch of open grassland surrounding a nicely refurbished log cabin. It sat alongside a narrow macadam road that wound its way into the surrounding mountains. The cabin was the size of a typical one-story home, with fresh chinking of some sort of white elastic material between the logs. An early twentieth century barn of heavy wooden planks sat adjacent to the cabin, it too appeared to be in excellent condition. The lawn surrounding both buildings was mowed to about four inches, unusual for a rustic cabin in the middle of nowhere.

A dead eight-point buck lay by the side of the cabin. It had been tagged and gutted.

"Whose deer?" said Pierce.

"Mine," Nando answered gingerly. He ran a hand through his hair and rubbed at the back of his neck as Pierce walked over to inspect the big game tag that had been attached to an ear. It had been properly completed with all the blanks filled in.

"Where'd you shoot this one?" asked Pierce.

"Way up the mountain," said Nando. "Nowhere near the camp. I can show you if you want."

I turned to Sal. "Why isn't your deer tagged? You do have a hunting license, don't you?"

Sal raised his palms in a gesture of appeal. "My license is on my other coat. I switched it for a light jacket when I went back for the deer. It was getting warm, and I perspire easily. Perhaps you noticed, huh?" He paused as if expecting me to answer. When I didn't, his face lit up and he turned to Deputy Pierce. "See? Your boss is a good man—but of course you know that already! He's being kind. He knows I'm too fat! Please. Everyone. Come into my cabin and I will present my license for you to inspect. Come!" he insisted. "Nando will prepare a fine meal for us!"

Nando opened the cabin door and stepped aside, bidding our entry with an outstretched arm. "After you, gentlemen?"

Pierce and I followed Sal inside. Nando shadowed us and closed the door behind him. The place was well kept and airy with spacious windows throughout. A gorgeous mahogany table was centered in the room surrounded by four sturdy wooden chairs. To our left, a large flat-screen TV rested on a wooden console. A plush leather sofa invited you to settle in and relax. The cabin contained three other rooms: two were bedrooms, the other a massive gourmet kitchen complete with a six-burner stainless gas range and large double oven.

Sal grabbed an orange hunting coat off the back of a chair and removed his hunting license from a side pocket. He handed it to me. "See! I'm completely legal."

20

As I looked over the license, Sal turned to his companion and said, "Nando, I promised the gentleman a nice Italian breakfast. Sausage and—"

"Thank you, really," I cut in, "but we don't have time."

Sal frowned, his plump lips forming a pout of genuine disappointment. "Coffee then?" he implored. "I have an excellent espresso!"

"Appreciate the offer," I told him, "but I want to take a walk with Nando. See where he shot his buck."

"I understand," said Sal. "You and your deputy are very busy men. But the walk where Nando hunts is long and the mountain steep. You will be thirsty when you return. I shall have a nice cold drink waiting for you."

I have to admit Sal's kind gestures were starting to soften my feelings toward him. You couldn't help but like the guy.

I hate when that happens.

As I was about to leave with Nando, I spotted a photograph lying on the mahogany table next to a pile of other pictures. It was from bygone days. A black and gray snapshot of an old and grizzled trapper cradling a lever-action rifle in his right arm while his foot rested comfortably atop the closed jaws of a huge steel-toothed bear trap. He had narrow, piercing eyes and a great white beard. He was standing next to a huge canine of mixed breed that appeared to be more wolf than dog. The creature was tethered to a tree stump by a heavy steel chain, its massive neck fitted with a sturdy leather collar. In the background stood a barn, its wood-planked sidewall lined with dozens of animal traps that hung in clusters by their chains. Being a trapper myself, I was immediately taken by it. Mesmerized, you might even say.

"Who's the man in the photograph?" I asked.

"I don't know, but that's my barn in the background," explained Sal. "I found the photograph in a drawer along with some old bills after I bought the place. It must have been taken a long time ago." He picked it off the pile and handed it to me.

I took the photo from him, my eyes poring over every detail. It was taken in the late eighteen hundreds but had been kept in near perfect condition. We were in Noxen Township, remote even by today's standards. Surrounded by a rugged area known as the Endless Mountains, the largely uninhabited forest extended north and west for a hundred miles. A large population of deer and black bears lived here. Rattlesnakes too. More rattlesnakes than people, in fact. I thought about the uninhabited, raw wilderness that existed back then and tried to envision what it was like to live in Pennsylvania's north woods as a hunter and trapper in those early days—

"You want it?"

I snapped out of my trance. "Excuse me?"

"The picture," offered Sal. "Take it, it's yours."

Had the proposal been made by an innocent friend or family member, I would have been delighted. I was fascinated with the photo—Sal could read it in my face—but I would never accept it. Police officers don't take gifts from people being investigated for criminal activity—especially while they're in the middle of the investigation.

"Why don't you send it over to the newspaper down town?" I suggested. "They're always looking for historical photos about life in Wyoming County." I handed it back to him, adding, "This one is really unique. I've never seen anything like it!"

Sal paused in thought for a moment before laying the photo back on the table. "Yeah. Sure," he said. "Maybe I will."

But he never did.


Nando and I started in the opposite direction of Sal's treestand and walked at a brisk pace a good half-mile from the cabin before he pointed to a fresh gut pile in the woods. "This is where he dropped," he said. "Got him another hundred yards uphill."

We were on a game trail that snaked its way to the top of the mountain, a narrow plateau at twenty-five-hundred feet. The woods were damp and thick here. Most of the trees still held their leaves, autumn's dazzling colors a sight to be seen. The sun had warmed the land considerably since my walk with Sal, and the deep, earthy sent of soil and decomposing leaves filled my senses.

From where we stood, I couldn't see anything that appeared to be out of order. No bait, no treestands, and no blinds. I walked over to the gut pile and sliced open the stomach, finding a thick, green gruel-like mixture of plant material inside. Unlike Sal's deer, this one hadn't been feeding on apples and corn, which meant Nando was in the clear with his kill.

As Nando and I made out way back down the mountain, I questioned him about Sal's deer, but he had little to say, claiming his involvement was merely to assist Sal in dragging the carcass back to camp, and that he had no idea where the deer had been shot.

When we stepped back into Sal's camp, I could smell coffee brewing, and two tall glasses of water had been set on the kitchen counter, fresh lemon wedges neatly fitted on their rims. I looked over at Deputy Pierce and shook my head, indicating no bait was found.

Sal walked from the kitchen to greet us, a steaming cup of black espresso in his hand. "Is everything good? No trouble with Nando's deer?"

"Yes," I said. "No trouble."

Nando lifted a glass from the counter. "Ice cold," he offered. "Straight from our well."

I accepted it, thirsty from our trek. It was unusually warm for an October day, and my throat was sandpaper. I watched Nando take the other glass and drink from it, then I drank too. I could feel the cold water coursing all the way down to my stomach. Sal watched in silence, wondering, I suppose, what would happen with his illegal kill. I finished the glass and set it back on the counter.

"Let's take a walk out back," I said. "See what we have."

Sal pressed his lips into a thin line. "Why bother? Like I said before: I have apples and corn out back, but I wasn't hunting near my cabin."

"Understood, but I'm going to take a look for myself. You can wait here or tag along, it's up to you."

"Please," insisted Sal, "don't misunderstand. I'm only trying to save you some time. It's the first day of archery season; surely you have other places to be. And, too, you must be tired from your journey with Nando. I can save you the walk! Yes! There is bait behind my cabin!"

"I want to see it." I opened the cabin door and stepped out with Pierce. Sal and Nando followed. I thought I might find a blood trail leading from the bait in the direction of the Sal's kill. It would certainly help my case, and hopefully end the entire matter.

We walked a short distance across the back lawn until we came to a series of ten steps made of fieldstone that led to a lower meadow. I could see apples lying in the grass, perhaps a hundred or more, as we descended. Moving closer, I came upon a good-sized spread of shelled corn that had been soaked with a thick brown coating. Adjacent to it, a fifty-

24

pound salt block containing a generous mix of corn kernels had been placed, the ground surrounding it worn bare from visiting deer, their tracks everywhere in the loose soil.

"What's the brown stuff on the corn?" I asked.

"Molasses!" said Sal. "Really brings them in."

I thought as much but wanted Sal to confirm it for me.

"I want to be sure I got this right," I said. "You put the food here to attract deer because you want to grow big antlers for the guide service you run, correct?"

Sal smiled at me. "Of course! I have many friends who enjoy hunting here. Family too! I want them to be happy. Without the food, they may never see a deer to shoot. And if they do, it might only be a small one. Such a pity. I want my friends to be successful—and proud! Not killers of little Bambi! How else can I be sure of this unless I feed the deer to make them big and strong?"

Remains of salt block with deer tracks in loose soil.

I nodded with feigned empathy and pulled a camera from my pocket. Sal's expression turned grave, suspecting that more picture-taking could only confirm trouble was brewing. I turned and snapped a photo of his cabin to indicate its proximity to the bait, then took several more pictures of the apples scattered about. Kneeling, I photographed a close-up

25

of the corn to illustrate its brown molasses coating, then I took a plastic sandwich bag from my pocket, scooped up some kernels, and dropped them inside. Sal and Nando stepped away to converse in low tones as I concluded my photo session with close-ups of the salt block and fresh deer tracks.

"Why are you so interested in the food I put out for the deer?" asked Sal. "I was at least a thousand feet away, at my treestand, when I took my shot."

"Even if you were two thousand feet away it would still be an illegal kill," I said. "You admit putting food out to attract deer into your property, and then you went out hunting for them. Your deer's stomach is packed with corn and apples—the same stuff you have behind your camp. It's obvious that it was feeding here. The baiting law has been on the books for decades, Sal. You should know better."

Sal frowned in thought. "Well, yes. Of course I know about the law. But how far away must I be to be legal?"

"There is no set distance."

"But that does not seem fair!"

Pierce stepped beside me and said, "It's done that way for a reason: if a distance were set, say a thousand feet like in your case, then all a hunter would have to do is be a thousand-and-one feet from the bait to be legal. That would essentially make hunting with bait lawful in Pennsylvania. We don't want that."

"So the warden gets to choose? He makes the law up in his head—like a whim with nothing in writing to guide him. I do not understand!"

I said, "It doesn't work that way, Sal. We take many things into consideration before making an arrest. A major factor is whether the hunter has knowledge of the bait, either because he stumbled upon it or because he put it there himself, as in your case." I paused and let him digest what I said. Then added, "Which means that Nando is just as liable as you are because he knew about the bait behind your cabin and helped you transport the deer."

Sal and Nando exchanged nervous glances. "But Nando is innocent, *I* killed the deer!"

"I haven't made up my mind about Nando, yet," I said.

"How much is the fine?" insisted Sal. "I'll pay, but you should not fine Nando."

"The fine is seven hundred dollars: five hundred for the illegal kill and two hundred for using bait."

He nodded, his face exuding a sense of submission that the matter was coming to a close.

"You can always take a hearing," I added, "tell your story to a judge."

"Oh, I don't want to do that," groaned Sal. He reached for his wallet. "I have money; can I pay the fine right now?"

He caught me off guard. Who goes hunting with seven hundred dollars cash in their pocket?—or did he think I took credit cards! And there was something else: something in his open gaze, his brow raised in question, that seemed to say, *How much will it take for you to walk away and forget the whole thing?*

There was a time when we would take fine money from violators to settle a case, provided they signed a legal document called a Field Acknowledgement of Guilt. But those days ended over a decade earlier.

"You can't pay me," I said. "But if you want to settle this, I can walk over to my vehicle and write two citations for your violations today. There's a section on the back of the citations where you can check-off that you're pleading guilty. Then you can mail them to the district justice along with your payment. Case closed."

"Of course!" he assured me. "Give me the papers. I will take care of it first thing tomorrow." He paused, dropping his brow in reservation. "And Nando, my goombah? What will become of him?"

I looked directly at Nando. "I want you to understand that you could be arrested for assisting Sal with an unlawfully killed deer. You both were in possession of the buck when Deputy Pierce showed up."

27

Nando swallowed hard and bowed his head, nodding in silence.

"I'm not going file charges against you, though. Not this time, anyway. We have one illegal deer, and there will only be one person fined. Besides, you've cooperated with me, and I'm taking that into account."

Sal's face lit up. He clapped his hands together in resounding approval. "Yes! I knew you were a good man!" Then, with a sly wink, he added, "—An honest man, too!"

I had to work pretty hard at keeping a straight face, considering his dubious compliment.

"Just trying to be fair," I said.

"It's an honorable thing that you do," said Sal. "Nando and I appreciate your kindness. But I have one concern: when I pay my fine, will I lose my license to hunt?"

"That decision is made in Harrisburg," I said. "It's not up to me."

In truth, because he had killed a baited deer, I was certain his license would be revoked. But we had orders from the top not to discuss revocation with anyone we arrested. When prosecution reports go to the front office, prior convictions can surface that are unknown to the arresting officer. A second offense will often result in the hunter being flagged for a period of license revocation.

Sal gave a dismissive shrug. "Fair enough. Hopefully the bosses in Harrisburg will take pity on me. Besides, I want to put this whole thing behind me—be done with it."

I started toward my patrol car for my citation box when Sal called out to me: "One more thing, warden?"

I stopped and turned around.

"The season is still young. May I continue to hunt?"

I thought about it. Sal had been pretty straight with me. Even though he was probably lying about where he shot the deer, he did admit killing it. He also confessed to putting out bait to lure deer into his property. In return, I was confiscating his trophy buck, he was going to lose his hunting license for at least a year, and he agreed to plead guilty and pay a hefty fine. What more could I ask?

"Never said I was going to write a ticket for failure to tag your deer, did I?"

"This is true."

"Well, you still have your tag, go ahead and hunt. Just not here—your property is baited."

Sal's eyebrows shot upward, his face a mask of bright anticipation. "And what if I remove the bait? I can do this today! Everything will be cleaned up!"

"If you clean it all up—and I mean every trace—by law, you can hunt here thirty days afterwards."

"Ah! This is good! Deer season will still be open."

Pierce and I walked back to Sal's camp and took possession of the deer, each grabbing an antler. Sal and Nando watched as we dragged the heavy carcass to the back of my patrol car, loaded it on my big game carrier, and strapped it down with heavy rubber bungee cords.

After securing the deer, I wrote two citations for Sal and handed them to him.

"This was all my fault!" confessed Sal. "I appreciate what you are doing for us. I have learned my lesson: no more food for the deer. I promise, too, that I won't forget your kindness, officer."


Three weeks later, I received a phone call from Wyoming County District Court stating that Salvatore Giovanni Vastolano had lawyered up after pleading not guilty on both citations. He'd requested a hearing, the judge promising she'd schedule the trial some time after deer season had closed, when I'd have more time to prepare my case.

I have to admit I was surprised. Snookered again, I thought gloomily. I've always had a tendency to trust people, take a man at his word. And with the news that Sal wanted a hearing, I began to doubt myself. Maybe I was just too naïve. I'd been certain that he had no intention of taking a hearing.

And I began to wonder whether he'd hired an attorney because some barroom lawyer had convinced him that I didn't have a case or if he had decided immediately after I declined his offer:

*Can I pay the fine right now?*

His question came back to me like a bad dream.

Did he start playing me when I refused to take his money? Promising to plead guilty and pay his fine the following day, thereby calculating that I'd allow him to keep his deer tag in return for his cooperation? Was he really that shrewd? Could he read me that well?

Or was it because he didn't want to risk having his license revoked? A revocation period would certainly be bad news for his guide business. Scratch that—it would be the end of his guide business, at least for a few years, and a huge disappointment for his "clients," who by his own admission were friends and family members—an additional embarrassment.

Another possibility, and I thought the most probable, was that he was a career poacher who'd been bragging for years about how he was always one step ahead of the game warden. Now he'd been caught. The humiliation too much to bear, he'd decided to take a hearing. If he won, his bragging rights would be preserved, even bolstered, perhaps, by the fact that he'd duped a judge too.

These were some of the questions that played at the edge of my mind as the first of what ultimately would be a series of three judicial trials came to light.

The first was scheduled before District Justice Patricia Robinson, a no-nonsense judge with plenty of courtroom experience. There were several district justices in the county; however, the majority of my hearings were held in Justice Robinson's court, as it covered the most heavily hunted portion of my four-hundred square mile district. This was good for me and bad for poachers, not to mention any defense attorney who tried to intimidate her. Those who did were quickly put in their place. Judge Robinson had a background in hunting and a thorough understanding of state game laws. She was also pro law enforcement, which didn't mean she handed out guilty verdicts like candy at Christmas, but if you did your homework and had all your ducks in a row (as she would often say), you stood an excellent chance of winning your case.

I had two rules when it came to arresting poachers: the first, write citations only for those I could win in court; the second, do everything ethically possible in order to achieve that win. If that meant spending days in front of my desk researching criminal law, legal opinions, and judicial procedures, along with preparing witnesses for their testimony, then so be it. I hated the idea of losing, especially when it meant the bad guy would get away with the indiscriminate killing of wildlife.

With this case, I had no civilian witnesses to prepare for their testimony—only my deputy and I would be testifying. I didn't have to worry about Pierce; he was an outstanding deputy with many years of experience, and he knew how to handle himself both inside and outside the courtroom. Besides, most of the testimony would come from me, since I had written the citations and was the officer in charge of the investigation.

I wondered what in the world Sal could say in his defense. He had admitted putting out the bait to lure deer into his property and to killing the ten-point buck we found him with that day. On its face, the case seemed like an easy win. But I also knew that when a defense lawyer gets involved, anything is possible. Sal's attorney would question everything I did—or didn't do—in my investigation. He'd be looking for any mistakes that I may have made as well as for loopholes in the law, and if he found anything, his client might just walk.

The trial was set for a Monday morning in March, months after the close of deer season. And when I saw that Sal had shown up with Nando that day, I got a bad feeling in my gut. Nando had been standing right next to Sal when Sal admitted shooting the deer; he could only hurt him with his testimony, so why bring him along?

They were standing in the courtroom lobby, waiting for their attorney to arrive when Pierce and I brushed by them on our way into the conference room. We were a half hour early. It was there that we would sit behind closed doors and go over our case. Kind of a warm-up before the game you might say.

We sat across from each other in the room at a round wooden table as I took my notes from a briefcase and looked them over. There would be no district attorney (DA) present. I'd face the defense attorney on my own. In those days, almost all Game Law violations were summary offenses, the lowest level of criminal violations under Pennsylvania law. Unlike in misdemeanors and felonies, offenders don't receive criminal records when they're convicted of a summary offense. As a result, the DA's office didn't bother with them unless the arresting officer requested it under special circumstances. Even then, assistance from the DA was iffy. I rarely asked for help, even though I'd prosecuted hundreds of cases.

I looked up from my notes at Pierce. "You ready?"

"Yep."

"Questions?"

Peirce nodded slowly, methodically. "I think Nando is here to cover for Sal."

"That's not a question."

"What I'm trying to say is, are *you* ready?"

"I think so. I mean, what can they say? We've got them cold, right?"

Pierce chuckled.

"What?" I asked, scowling.

His face turned serious. Then he shrugged. "Now *you're* asking *me*! I just thought that was funny."

It always amazed him when I sought his advice. In Jeff's mind, I could do no wrong. The greatest game warden that ever lived. But I knew better. Jeff had a special insight about him, and at times, his most subtle observations would help me solve a complicated case. I watched him lean back in his chair and lace his fingers together in thought for a moment. Then he said, "Sal didn't bring Nando along to hold his hand while he pleads guilty in front of his attorney. Sal plans to testify, which means he intends to lie about something. And Nando is here to back him up."

"That would be a surprise," I said. "They came across as pretty decent guys back at their camp. Besides, I gave both men a huge break. Nando could've been arrested for assisting Sal with the deer, and he knows it. And I let Sal keep his tag. I think Sal is going to plead for mercy from the court. Nando might be here for moral support, but I can't believe they would both perjure themselves. They admitted to everything in front of both of us."

Pierce eyed me critically. He wasn't buying it.

I shrugged. "Whatever. No way they can win this." I pulled two documents from my briefcase and set them on the table. "Not with these."

"Court opinions on the Clod case?" said Pierce.

"Yep."

I didn't have to explain anything more to him. He'd been with me all the way through the investigation with Cletus Clod. The man had killed a bear up on Dutch Mountain several years ago. The camp where he was staying as a guest had been heavily baited, and although he was eight hundred feet from the bait when he shot his bear, Judge Robinson still found him guilty. Clod appealed her decision to the Wyoming County Court of Common Pleas, where his conviction was confirmed. He appealed once again, this time to the Commonwealth Court of Pennsylvania, where the case against him was upheld. I had written opinions from both appeals. The way I figured it, if Clod was found guilty for hunting with bait at a distance of eight hundred feet, Sal would be in serious trouble, considering that he shot his deer only a couple hundred feet farther away. By his own admission, he was hunting a thousand feet from the apples and corn at his camp.

There came a soft tapping on the door. "They're ready," called a female voice. It was the judge's clerical assistant, basically giving me a three-minute warning.

"Be right out," I said.

That's when the butterflies started swirling in my stomach. Although I'd prosecuted dozens of cases before, I still got nervous whenever I walked into a courtroom. Maybe because I cared so much. Too much, perhaps. Winning meant everything to me. We were in a rural county where word traveled at light speed. And if a poacher beats you in court, people hear about it. He brags to his friends, and they tell *their* friends. And soon the entire county knows. This concerned me, especially regarding bait cases, where a loss could open the door for every poacher for miles around who wanted to hunt over bait.

In rural America, a game warden's reputation can be made or unmade in a matter of weeks—days sometimes. I had a reputation of being fair but firm with the outlaws I'd met over the years. And the judge knew me as a dedicated officer who always presented a solid case—a tough man to beat in court. I aimed to keep that reputation intact.

I didn't know the defense attorney. He was from outside the county, one of hundreds lurking about. Some were no better than the criminals they defended. Thugs with briefcases who would do anything to win. Others weren't so bad. Likeable, in fact. Still, most defense attorneys seemed to use intimidation and bewilderment as a common strategy. And they came after you with one purpose in mind: to destroy you in court. Their job was to dismantle your case, and if that meant turning your witnesses into babbling fools, that would be just fine. As for me, they would scrutinize every facet of my investigation. Did I dot all my i's and cross all my t's, did I read the defendant his rights, intimidate him, bully him, pressure him into a confession? They'd look for anything that would indicate I overextended my authority. After all, the best defense is a good offense, especially when you can't win based on the merits of your case. Oh, you could beat them at their game all right. But you had to know where your case was weak. You looked at your evidence and your witnesses and your testimony, and you thought about how a defense attorney would attack each of them. Then you strengthened any weak points so he couldn't get the best of you. Besides, you had one thing on your side that a criminal defense attorney could never have, the most important thing of all: and that was the truth. And if you didn't have it, you deserved to lose.

I stood and began stuffing my paperwork back into my briefcase. Pierce got up and stepped around me and opened the door. We walked a short distance down a narrow corridor until we came to a second door. A sign said DISTRICT COURT. Pierce opened the door and followed me inside.

The place wasn't much bigger than the average two-car garage, with the judge's heavy wooden desk situated at the far wall as we entered. Sal and Nando sat with their attorney behind a wooden table that faced the judge's desk to her right. My deputy and I took seats at an identical table to her left. Behind us were several rows of folding chairs for any spectators who might be present. Today there were none.

Pierce and I stood from our seats when Judge Patricia Robinson entered the courtroom from a side door and approached her bench. Sal and Nando didn't take the hint and sat on their rumps. Their lawyer quickly stood, impatiently motioning them up with a sharp nod.

She was in her early forties. Tall, blonde, and attractive, even when donned in a plain black judge's robe. But her comeliness and graceful stride belied her no-nonsense demeanor. Judge Robinson eased herself into a large, well-upholstered chair and began to examine two citations on her desk as we reclaimed our seats. After reviewing the papers, she cast her gaze upon the defendant for a moment, then read the charges aloud and asked how he would plea.

"Not guilty, Your Honor."

She turned her head toward me. "Is the Commonwealth ready?"

"Yes, Your Honor. The Commonwealth calls Deputy Jeff Pierce."

I wanted Pierce to testify first because it was his initial discovery of the bait that had started everything in motion. He got up from his chair, walked over to Judge Robinson's desk, and raised his right hand. After being sworn in, he sat in a straight-backed wooden witness chair to the judge's immediate left and faced the courtroom.

In an attempt to keep things brief and to the point, I asked him a few questions about the bait at Sal's camp and then moved to his discovery of Sal and Nando with the ten-point buck. Pierce testified that Sal admitted killing the deer with a crossbow and that he also acknowledged putting bait behind his camp to attract deer.

When I finished with my questions, the defense attorney stood from his chair to begin his cross-examination of Deputy Pierce. I expected a lengthy interrogation, but instead he asked him one simple question: what distance from a baited area must a hunter be in order to avoid violating state game laws? When Pierce explained that the law provided no specific area or set distance, the attorney thanked him for his answer and sat down.

And that pretty much told me what his defense would be: the law was vague and unfair because there was no "line in the sand" telling hunters how far they had to be from a bait pile in order to hunt legally.

I was ready for it, and would address the question later in the trial.

Next to take the stand, I testified at length about Sal's admission that he killed the deer (being careful along the way to point a finger at Sal and verbally identify him as the defendant—a requirement in every criminal trial lest you risk having the case dismissed), including the fact that after I told him he'd be cited for killing a deer over bait, he asked if he could "pay the fine right now." I testified further that Sal told me he'd been baiting his camp for the past ten years to grow big antlers for his guide service, and that the stomach of the deer he'd killed was packed to the bursting point with partially digested corn, the likes of which I'd never seen in more than twenty-five years as a game warden. I also told the judge about Sal's refusal to show me where the deer was standing when he shot it, making it difficult for me to believe that he'd killed the animal by his treestand. During my lengthy testimony, I entered the dozens of photographs I'd taken of the apples, the molasses-covered corn, and the salt block into evidence, presenting them one-by-one to the judge along with with copies for the defense attorney. I also testified that I did not arrest Sal's hunting companion, Nando, for taking advantage of the bait at the cabin because his deer had been killed a half-mile away, and that my examination of the stomach contents revealed that no corn or apples had been present.

When I finished, the defense attorney did a softball cross-examination of my testimony. He realized I had my bases covered and there was nothing he could do to trip me up. Besides, his client was about to take the stand in his own defense.

When he did, I was astounded by what he had to say.

After being duly sworn by Judge Robinson, Salvatore Giovanni Vastolano calmly took his seat in the witness chair and began to lie through his teeth. He began by testifying that he'd climbed up into his treestand to wait for a deer to come by, and when he finally saw one (here he was sure to emphasize that the deer was running in the opposite direction of his camp), he took a shot with his crossbow. I felt my jaw drop when he said this. Sal's treestand hadn't been used in years. He knew I was aware of this. And he had told me that because he was "too old and too fat" to climb, he'd been standing at the base of the tree when he shot at a deer—how could he sit there and lie under oath like this?

With growing amazement, I listened as he went on to say that he and Nando attempted to locate a blood trail, but, unable to find one, decided to return to camp when they happened to stumble upon a freshly killed ten-point buck along the way. Not knowing who shot it or where it came from, they decided to keep the deer. After all, why let a perfectly good animal go to waste?

At first I wasn't sure why he'd lied about being up in his treestand when he took a shot at the deer. Then it came to me: he knew the deer we found him with, the very deer he now claimed he discovered dead on his property, had a wound from a broadhead that went through its body in a horizontal plane—impossible if it had been hit from above. Sal put himself in a treestand because he didn't want to leave any question in the judge's mind that he might have been the person who shot it.

Looking at me with a narrow eye, he continued to testify under oath, stating that he had insisted on taking me back to his treestand to show me where the deer had been, but I refused to walk back with him. He also testified that he had put the apples and a salt block behind his cabin but denied that he'd been doing it for the past ten years and that he ran a guide service for hunters. And, incredibly, he said he never wanted to plead guilty to killing the deer we found him with, testifying instead that I had bullied him into it, chanting, "You're guilty, you're guilty, you're guilty," until he finally broke down and offered to pay his fine just to get me off his back.

But Sal made a fatal mistake in his deceitful testimony by admitting under oath that he'd put bait behind his cabin. I suppose he did this because the bait was on his property, and it would have been pretty hard to convince even the most sympathetic and gullible of judges that someone else had put it there. But Sal and his attorney figured they were far enough away from the bait as long as the judge believed he'd been hunting from his treestand, a distance of more than three football fields, when he shot at a deer.

When Sal finished testifying, Nando took the stand and parroted everything he said. I have to admit, I never expected this. I'd heard defendants lie in court before, but in all my years, never as flagrantly as these two.

The trial ran all morning long until it was finally time for closing arguments by the prosecution and the defense. It would be our last opportunity to clinch the verdict we had each strived for—guilty for me, not guilty for the defense. In truth, we both figured that she had probably come to a conclusion at some point in the trial. Still, there remained a glimmer of optimism in each of us that whatever we said in these final minutes might win her over. For neither of us could be certain which side she favored.

The defense always goes first in summation arguments, and when Judge Robinson called Sal's attorney for his final words, he stood from his seat and told the court that everything about the case boiled down to a question of proof—asking her to find his client not guilty for a variety of reasons, not the least of which was that the Commonwealth could not prove that Sal had killed the ten-point buck—or any other deer for that matter. He went on to argue that his client was hunting a thousand feet away from the bait at his camp, with his back to the cabin. He could not see the bait from the treestand, and therefore could not be guilty of using it for the purpose of hunting. He added that in addition to these facts, the law pertaining to hunting with bait was unconstitutional because it wasn't defined clearly enough to enable an individual with ordinary intelligence to know how far away from the baited area he must be to hunt lawfully. To bolster this argument, he used my own words against me by stating that I had told his client I would have arrested him even if he'd been *two* thousand feet from the bait, asserting the law was unfair in its ambiguity. In closing, he stated that we never saw Sal place the bait, nor did we see deer feeding in the baited area, and that we failed to prove specifically where the deer was located when it was shot and from what direction the deer had come, stating further that, assuming *arguendo*, even if his client knew of the bait, he could not take advantage of it because he was more than a thousand feet away and his crossbow only had an effective distance of thirty yards.

I had to admit, Sal got his money's worth from his attorney.

In return, I stood and argued that the Game Code clearly prohibits hunting with bait as an enticement for game or wildlife, which includes, by definition, taking advantage of any such baited area. I reminded the judge that the defendant had admitted killing the ten-point buck to my deputy and to me when we found him in possession of the animal, even though he denied it in court today. I added that even if she wanted to discount his admission that he'd killed the deer, the defendant had nevertheless admitted in this very court that he had put food on his property to attract deer and that he was hunting within a thousand feet of it.

"Your Honor," I continued, "in this very court, you heard a similar case in recent years: In *Commonwealth v. Clod*, a baiting violation which happened to take place two miles from the defendant's property, a hunter shot and killed a bear eight hundred feet from a baited camp very similar to the scenario in the case at hand. As you may recall, Mr. Clod was convicted in this court, and he subsequently appealed to the Court of Common Pleas where your conviction was upheld by Judge Brendan Vanston. Mr. Clod appealed once again to the Commonwealth Court of Pennsylvania, where his conviction was affirmed for a second time by a panel of three judges.

"And now we have Mr. Salvatore Vastolano," I said, turning to the defendant, "who claims to have been hunting one thousand feet from his camp—a camp that he deliberately baited to attract game. What if we never considered the fact that my deputy and I found him in possession of a ten-point buck that he admitted killing that day? What if we simply took him at his word—that he was hunting in a treestand one thousand feet away from bait that he intentionally placed to attract game when he shot at a deer with his crossbow? As stated, Cletus Clod was eight hundred feet from his baited cabin when he shot a bear and was convicted of hunting with bait. The defendant testified that he was hunting two hundred feet farther away from his baited cabin than Mr. Clod. Does another two hundred feet make any difference whatsoever? The Commonwealth thinks not."

I sat down. "Commonwealth rests, Your Honor."

There was nothing else I could say. I felt confident I would win. No doubt, Sal was guilty—after all, he had admitted killing the ten-pointer to Deputy Pierce and me. Now he had come to court to swear under oath that he merely found the deer dead on his property. Worse, his companion Nando had backed up his false testimony. But none of that mattered now. The trial was over. I gave it my best shot, and it all came down to what the judge thought. Had I convinced her beyond a reasonable doubt that Sal was guilty? Or would she rule in his favor? I tried to read her as she sat behind her desk, busily sorting through the notes she had taken, but she left me no clue.

Soon she paused and looked up at the attorney, her gaze steady and impassive. Then her eyes withdrew from him and set dead level on Salvatore Vastolano. "I've made my decision," she said, glancing my way briefly before fixing a penetrating glare on the defendant. "Mr. Vastolano, I have found your testimony to be incredible. There is absolutely no doubt in my mind that you are guilty. The officers testified that you admitted putting bait at your camp to attract deer into your property. Then you told them that you killed the deer that they found you with—a deer whose stomach contained the same food items that were discovered at your cabin."

Now her eyes cooled as they focused on the defense attorney once more. "Counselor," she said, "I've taken into consideration your argument that the section your client is charged under is vague, and therefore unconstitutional. I disagree. The Pennsylvania Game and Wildlife Code states that it is unlawful to take advantage of any food or bait while hunting, and that is clearly what happened here."

Judge Robinson had taken everything into consideration with her verdict, telling Sal to his face, basically, that she didn't believe his story about finding a dead deer on his property. Nor did she buy his attorney's argument that the law was unclear. She ordered him to pay the fine and court costs in full and added a four-year revocation period of his hunting privileges to her sentence, prompting Sal to immediately appeal his conviction to the Court of Common Pleas (Wyoming County trial court) where his case would be heard anew.

Three months later, Salvatore Giovanni Vastolano's second trial was heard before President Judge Brendan J. Vanston, his defense attorney arguing, once again, that the Commonwealth could not prove that he had killed a deer, nor could we prove that he had taken advantage of the food at his camp because it was too far away.

After hearing arguments during a lengthy court battle, the trial judge found Salvatore Vastolano guilty as charged and issued a written opinion that stated, in part, as follows: *The defendant testified that the location from which he shot at the deer was more than a thousand feet from the location of the bait, and that he could not see the bait from the treestand.*

*He concluded, therefore, that he could not be guilty of using the bait to kill this particular deer. Such a conclusion is absurd. The evidence in this case proved beyond a reasonable doubt that the defendant was aware of the baited area, and that the deer he shot (this, by his own admission) was headed in the general direction of the bait when he shot it. Further, the evidence shows beyond any doubt that the deer in question had recently sampled the very same bait. Consequently, any protestation that he was at some considerable distance from the bait is irrelevant. As a result, he is found guilty of all charges.*

Sal wasted no time filing a second appeal, only this time it would be heard before the Commonwealth Court of Pennsylvania (an appellate court that is one step under the Supreme Court), where his attorney hoped to have the verdict overturned by a new three-judge panel. I waited more than a year for a decision from the higher court, and when it finally came down, Sal's conviction was affirmed in a seven-page written opinion.

In its conclusion, the Court found as follows: *First, because we assume that people are free to steer between lawful and unlawful conduct, we insist that laws give the person of ordinary intelligence a reasonable opportunity to know what is prohibited, so that he may act accordingly. Contrary to Vastolano's assertion, the fact that the statute fails to contain a precise mathematical distance from the bait is not enough to render the statue void for vagueness. The extent of a 'baited area' is defined only by the capacity of bait placed anywhere within it to act as a lure for the hunter. An arbitrary spatial limitation would fail to protect those animals that are attracted within shooting range by bait in areas just outside the limitation.*

*Additionally, here, it is clear from reading the Game Code that a hunter is prohibited from using or taking advantage of any type of bait or other food to hunt game. Because such language gives the hunter of ordinary intelligence a reasonable opportunity to know the difference between lawful and unlawful conduct so that he may act accordingly, the provision is not unconstitutionally vague, either on its face or as applied. Similarly, because the key to determining one's guilt under the statute is whether one took advantage of the baited area, rather than one's distance from the bait, the statute does not promote arbitrary enforcement as Vastolano claims.*

*Next, Vastolano argues that the evidence adduced at the trial is insufficient to support his convictions. He points out that both convictions depend on a finding that he used bait to hunt and possess a deer. Vastolano argues that the Commonwealth failed to prove that he had any knowledge of the bait or that he had any intent to take advantage of the bait. Vastolano also argues that the Commonwealth did not offer direct evidence of any of the elements of the crime and, thus, did not prove each and every element of the crime beyond a reasonable doubt. We disagree.*

*Although no direct evidence [evidence based on a witness's personal knowledge or observation] was offered, here, there is circumstantial evidence [evidence that generates a conclusion by reasoning drawn from facts known about a case] to establish beyond a reasonable doubt that Vastolano used bait to hunt for and possess a deer in violation of the Game Code. The trial court found incredible Vastolano's testimony that he did not know about the bait and did not take advantage of it. Indeed, Vastolano admitted that he had been feeding the deer for ten years and that the apples, corn and salt and mineral blocks were on land owned by him. Vastolano also admitted killing the deer. Further, the evidence supports the trial court's finding that the deer had recently sampled the bait. Because this evidence supports a finding that the defendant took advantage of the bait at his camp to hunt a deer, his convictions must stand, and we affirm the order of the trial court.*

I was thankful for the ruling, for it turned out to be an important legal opinion, not just for me but also for every game warden in Pennsylvania, because it's a judicial decision that can be used as a standard in baiting cases throughout the entire Commonwealth for years to come.

Sal didn't appeal his case any further (i.e. the Supreme Court). Instead, he paid his seven hundred dollar fine (maximum at the time) and lost his Pennsylvania hunting and trapping privileges for four years. I have no idea what his legal fee was, but it had to be well into the thousands of dollars considering that his attorney had represented Sal in three separate court hearings.

Those days have long since passed, and Salvatore Giovanni Vastolano, after serving his revocation period, continues to hunt from his camp in the mountains of Wyoming County with his friend Nando. He no longer uses bait to lure game into his property, and can often be found puttering around his cabin while his friends and family are back in the woods, hunting for deer.

Another game warden has taken my place since then. He often drives past Sal's cabin on his way to patrol the mountains. I hear Sal goes out of his way to offer him a hearty hand wave and a friendly smile when he sees him.

I would expect nothing less.

# Voice in the Wilderness

IN MY EARLY DAYS as a game warden, I was assigned
to the southeast region of the state with a patrol district that
included Philadelphia County. In those days, there were still
a few large tracts of land in northern Philadelphia where
hunters could be found; however, most of my patrols were
restricted to rural sections of neighboring Montgomery
County. The only time I ever set foot in Philadelphia was if
called in for an investigation, which seemed to happen with
far too much frequency.

I remember well the buck season of nineteen seventy-six
when I received information from regional headquarters
about a Philadelphia resident suspected of killing a doe
ninety miles north in Schuylkill County. A witness reported
seeing him drag the deer out of the woods and put it into the
trunk of his car. He wrote down the license number as the
hunter sped off, then drove to a nearby diner and used a
payphone in the lobby. Dropping a dime into the coin slot, he
dialed the number for the Pennsylvania Game Commission
and relayed the information to a dispatcher who promptly
called me at my house, where I had just stopped for lunch.

"Did the informant leave a return number?" I asked.

"I tried to get one but he refused," said the dispatcher.

"Is he sure it was a doe and not a short-horned buck?"

"Said he was."

"Did you get a description of the hunter?"

"Black—about six three, two hundred fifty pounds or so. I
ran the tag. Name's Junior Roosevelt. Drives a seventy-one
Pontiac Catalina. Gold with a black vinyl top. Said he

watched him pick up the deer and put it in his trunk like it was nothing."

"Small doe, huh?"

"That's the thing. He says the deer was pretty big. Maybe a hundred and fifty pounds."

"Can't wait to meet the guy."

"Figured as much. I got his address and phone number for you. He was headed for the turnpike. Probably halfway back to Philly by now."

I copied the information and hung up. He was right. The suspect was probably on his way home, which gave me less than two hours to intercept him.

I had several Philadelphia deputies who knew the city well. In Pennsylvania, deputies are paid volunteers who hold down regular jobs outside the agency while working for the Game Commission on a part-time basis. Deputy Al Lange was off from work that day, so I gave him a call and arranged to meet him at a grocery store parking lot near the county line.

It was late afternoon, and we planned to confront our suspect when he returned home. Because my marked patrol car would have been easily detected, we took Lange's personal vehicle and drove through the gray, congested city for a good half hour until we finally arrived at Roosevelt's house. It was a small two-story row home built of bricks, typical of other homes in the area. Cars were parked bumper-to-bumper up and down the narrow street, but we managed to find a spot where Lange could squeeze his vehicle between two parked cars just a few doors from our suspect.

By seven o'clock, I started to worry. He should have been home by now. The sun had set a while ago, and every time headlights approached, we peered into the cold, dark night with strained eyes hoping they belonged to our suspect's Pontiac. Most folks were home by then, lights glowing warmly in their windows as they prepared to sit down for dinner and relax in front of the TV. I envied them.

Lange unscrewed the lid from his thermos and poured some hot coffee into it.

"Hungry?" he asked.

"Little. Why?"

"Sounds like an alley cat crawled inside your stomach."

He leaned past me and opened the glove box for a spare cup. Lange poured some coffee into it and handed it to me. Then he reached into the back seat and grabbed a lunch pail. "I brought enough for both of us."

I smiled in amazement. Nine kids at home and he was still thinking about someone else when he packed his dinner.

"Hope you don't mind peanut butter and jelly," he said, handing me a sandwich wrapped in cellophane.

"One of my favorites."

The hours dragged on until midnight with no sign of our poacher. Deputy Lange still had to get to his regular job in the morning, so I called off the surveillance and we went back for my vehicle. I asked him to swing by and check for the suspect's car on his way to work. He assured me he would.


When the phone rang, I was jolted awake from a dead sleep. I checked my watch: four in the morning. Expecting to hear Deputy Lange's voice, I groped in the dark for the receiver and picked up.

"Bill, it's Harry." His voice was grim. "I have a problem."

It was Deputy Scuron from Philadelphia County. "What's wrong?" I asked.

"I'm in a house with a deer inside. You should see the place. The television is in pieces, lights are knocked over—the place looks ransacked!"

My mind was spinning, trying to process what I'd just heard. "Where? What house?" I croaked, standing at the edge of my bed.

"Fairmount Park. A deer jumped through a window and landed in bed with two elderly people. Dogs must have been chasing it. It's in the living room right now, and there's blood everywhere!"

"Are you okay?"

"Yes, but the old couple went to the hospital for treatment. The deer has a broken leg and it's standing here looking at me. The police are here too, Bill. They want me to do something. Do you have your tranquilizer gun?"

My heart sank knowing I was miles away and couldn't help. "It's in the shop for repairs," I said regretfully. "You have your handgun with you, right?"

"Yeah, but—"

"Look, I'd hate to be in your shoes right now but the deer has to be put down before it causes more damage or ends up hurting somebody else. You don't have a choice; you're going to have to shoot it."

There was a long silence on the other end.

"Harry? Are you there?"

"Yeah. Sorry. The deer just ran headfirst into a wall. Cracked the wallboard and hit a two-by-four stud so hard the house shook. I thought it might have been knocked out but it's starting to get back up. Hold on—"

I heard him put the receiver down. There was a muffled shot, followed seconds later by a throng of muddled voices. I waited for my deputy to pick up the phone, seconds ticking away forever before he finally returned.

"I got him, Bill," he breathed. "He stood up and stared at me, looking kind of dazed. I shot him in the head. The police are carrying the carcass out right now."

I let out a sigh of relief. "Good job, Harry."

"Thanks. I just hope the elderly couple are okay."

"Yeah. Me too."

"Well, if you don't need me for anything, I guess I'll head home."

"Look, we're both wide awake," I said. "How 'bout I get into a uniform and meet you for breakfast. Had a doe shot in Schuylkill County yesterday. We might be able to catch up with the guy later this morning."

49

**B**uilt in the early thirties, the Mayfair Diner, a train-car style eatery with a stainless façade, is a Philadelphia landmark best known for its home-style breakfasts and tasty deserts. When I walked in, Deputy Scuron was sitting in a window booth way at the back staring at the traffic lined up on Frankfort Avenue, a cup of steaming coffee on the table in front of him. He looked up and waved me over.

People turned in their seats to gawk as I passed in full uniform. They knew I was no city cop; their uniforms were blue, not green. State cop, park ranger, border patrol…bus driver. Who knew? I was a walking enigma.

When I reached Scuron's table, I pulled off my jacket and slid into a vinyl-covered bench seat opposite him. From out of nowhere, a middle-aged waitress in a fifties-style pink outfit hovered over us attentively. "Coffee?"

I ordered mine black. She handed me a menu. "Waffles and eggs on special today."

"Sold," I said. I nodded toward Scuron. "He'll have scrapple with two eggs over and rye toast. Easy on the butter."

She looked at my deputy and smiled. "Does he always do that?"

"What?"

"Order for you?"

"Only when he's buying, which isn't often."

She nodded sympathetically, then took a pen from an apron pocket, eyes flicking to the patch on my shoulder as she scribbled our orders on a notepad. "Game Commission?" she remarked. "What kind of games do you play?"

*Only in Philadelphia*, I thought drearily. I glanced at Scuron. He rolled his eyes in empathy knowing how much I hated being in the city.

"We're game wardens," I said.

She looked at me, her parted lips and squinty stare confirming her bewilderment.

"We arrest wildlife poachers."

"Oh?" She paused for a moment, then said, "A little out of your territory, huh?"

It was only the umpteenth time I'd heard someone say that since I'd been assigned here a year ago. I willed a thin smile and nodded. She smiled back, then turned toward the kitchen with our orders.

"Quite an ordeal with the deer earlier," I said to Scuron.

He shook his head somberly. "I feel sorry for the old couple. They both had broken bones. They're hurting pretty bad. And the house—man, it's a wreck!" He paused for a moment. "Got the scare of my life, too."

"I can imagine. That was a lot of pressure having to shoot a deer inside someone's home."

He nodded. "True enough. But it was *after* I shot the deer that I really got concerned."

"What do you mean?"

"I saw a window shade flutter—walked over for a look and there was a bullet hole in it. All I could think about was the other homes out there that might have been hit. I felt sick. I lifted the shade expecting to see a hole in the window, but my bullet was lying on the sill. It hit the window and dropped straight down. Never put a mark on it."

"Thank God!"

"That's what I thought, too."

Our waitress floated over to our table and set a cup and saucer in front of me. With coffee pot in hand, she filled my cup and then freshened Scuron's. "Breakfast will be ready in a jiff," she said, then glided to the next table with her pot.

Suddenly my handheld radio came alive: *"Headquarters to six-three-zero!"*

I keyed the mike. "Go ahead."

"We got a message from Deputy Lange. He said to tell you that the robin has returned to its roost."


A search warrant was out of the question. We were in the city, which would make it all but impossible to obtain due to the congested court system. Dealing with Philadelphia judges had been a problem for me in the past, too. I had recently served an arrest warrant on a city man, and when I brought my shackled prisoner before the judge, he looked at me as if I had two heads. I was in full uniform, badge on my chest, arrest warrant in my hand, and he still asked me for identification! I suspected that he never saw a game warden before that day, and doubted my authority.

I had to come up with a plan that would keep us away from the Philadelphia courts. Besides, all we had was a tip from an anonymous caller; that wouldn't be enough for a search warrant on Junior Roosevelt's car or house no matter what city we were working in. And I didn't expect him to admit he killed an illegal deer if I knocked on his door and asked him about it, either.

I needed a confession, and I had an idea that I thought might work.

Junior Roosevelt lived only a few blocks away. I instructed Scuron to drive to his house in his unmarked vehicle and park someplace close by. Once he was set up, he was to contact me by radio. The dispatcher had given me Junior's phone number and there was a phone booth in the lobby of the diner. If my idea worked, before long, our suspect would be out checking inside his trunk.

I asked the waitress for our bills and went to the cashier while Scuron got in his car and drove toward Junior's place. Within fifteen minutes, Scuron radioed that he was on location. I was standing by the pay phone and dropped a dime in the slot. I waited for a dial tone then called Junior's number, hoping he'd pick up. He did on the third ring.

"Hello?"

"Is this Junior Roosevelt?"

"Yes."

"This is Officer Wasserman with the Pennsylvania Game Commission. I have information that you shot a doe in Schuylkill County yesterday."

"Doe!" he yelped. "No sir. Not me!"

"I have an eyewitness who watched you drag the deer out of the woods and place it into your trunk," I said. "I'd like to stop by and talk to you about it."

There was a long pause. "Look, I ain't got nothin' in my trunk. I was hunting upstate yesterday, sure enough—but I never fired a shot. Whoever told you I got a deer, done got me confused with somebody!"

"Then you wouldn't mind if I checked the exterior of your car for blood stains or looked inside your trunk?"

Another pause. "You mean right now?"

"I'm not far away. I can be there in less than an hour."

A long pause. "Well...I guess that would be okay. But I got no deer in my trunk!"

"Appreciate that," I said. "See you soon."

As soon as I hung up, Junior hustled out the front door and over to his car. Deputy Scuron was sitting in his personal vehicle parked across the street. He watched Junior pause a moment and hunch over the rear bumper to look for blood stains. Scuron exited his vehicle and moved fast, approaching Junior from behind just as he opened his trunk.

"Mr. Roosevelt!" called Scuron.

Junior whipped around and faced him. He was immense. Massive shoulders swelled inside his coat, stretching the material taut. Scuron stopped abruptly, keeping a safe distance between them. "State Game Warden," he said. "I'd like to take a look at your car."

Junior's face fell into an expression of sheer puzzlement. "But you said on the phone that you were an hour away!"

Scuron stepped closer. "What's in the trunk?"

"Nothing," said Junior, backing away. "Look for yourself."

Scuron stepped closer and peered inside. The trunk was completely empty. The vehicle looked as though it had been washed and the trunk vacuumed. Junior must have been double-checking to be sure he'd left no evidence behind.

Scuron said, "If there's nothing in there, what are you looking for?"

Junior's brow crinkled in a frown of thought. "Ah…I was just checking to make sure I didn't forget something."

"Like what?"

"I was hunting up north. Thought I might have left something, that's all."

"Where's the doe you killed?"

"Like I said on the phone, I didn't kill no doe. I didn't kill nothin' at all."

Junior closed the trunk and glanced over at his house. "Come on," he said. "You can look in my house if you want. I ain't got nothing to hide. Then maybe you'll leave me alone."

Deputy Scuron trailed the big man down the narrow city sidewalk to his front door. Because he'd invited him to look, he didn't expect to find anything. But it would give him a chance to ask more questions, maybe trap him in a lie. Junior opened the door and ducked inside. Scuron followed, reaching up to brush the top of the doorframe with his fingertips as he entered.

Ten weeks passed, and Junior Roosevelt's case was a distant memory. We never found a shred of evidence that day. Junior allowed Scuron to look in his kitchen and his basement for deer meat. Even let him check his freezer. Nothing.

It had been a busy season, and I had several complicated deer cases scheduled for court that month. Unlike Junior's incident, where we only had the word of an unknown informant and no physical evidence, my other cases had witnesses who were prepared to testify in court against poachers I had arrested. Attorneys would be present, and I was up to my elbows in paperwork when the phone rang.

I picked up, distracted in thought. "Hello…?"

"Is this the game warden," asked a voice on the other end. He sounded young, perhaps in his twenties.

"Yes. Can I help you?"

"No, but I thought I might be able to help *you*."

"How's that?"

"I'm calling about a man named Junior Roosevelt. He's my uncle."

I straightened in my chair. "Okay. Go ahead."

"I was playing poker with him and his buddies last night. After a while, they started talking about a deer my uncle killed. I guess the whiskey loosened their tongues. It really upset me. What they did, I mean. Especially my uncle being a part of it."

I said. "We had information that he killed a doe during the December buck season. Is that what this is about?"

"Buck or doe, don't matter to me. It's the killing period! I hate it. Uncle Roosevelt was laughing about how he shot that poor creature. God's creation. Made my blood run cold. He laughed about how he fooled the game warden too. Guess that'd be you, right?"

"He didn't fool me," I said a little too defensively. "We just didn't have enough evidence to make an arrest. We never found the deer, and we don't have a witness. That is, unless you're willing to come forth."

"No sir," he said. "I can't do that. I mean, testify against a family member. But I'll tell you what I know. It's considerable. And after that, you can do with it what you want."


Later that evening, I telephoned Junior Roosevelt explaining that his case was reopened because an eyewitness had given me additional information about the deer.

"Wh...witness? What witness?" he stammered.

"I'm also filing charges against the three men you split the deer meat with," I said, spitting out their names rapid-fire.

"Whoa! Wait a minute, boss man. I don't know how you found out about them, but I guess you got me pretty good.

You right. I admit I killed a deer and I done wrong. But my friends…they innocent. Why you coming after them?"

"Because you gave them deer meat from your unlawful kill, and they accepted it."

There was a long, drawn-out sigh followed by an eternity of silence. Junior was slowing coming unraveled. I could almost hear the frantic whisperings of his mind.

Finally, he said, "You right. I done gave away all that meat. I don't like the taste of it." He let out a bark of nervous laughter. "Man o day! If this don't beat all!" Then, in a voice edged with pain, he added, "But I don't want my friends to get in trouble, boss man. This all my doin.'"

"It's too late. They already are."

"But I killed the deer. Can't you keep them out of this? They didn't ask me to do it. I did it on my own. They don't even hunt."

"Are you telling me you're willing to plead guilty?"

"Yes sir, boss man. Just asking that you keep my friends out of this."

It was all I needed to hear. One deer had been killed illegally, and I was satisfied with a single fine. "I'll see what I can do," I said.

Later that week, I drove to Junior Roosevelt's house and met with him. He gave me a full written statement explaining how he killed a doe in closed season and then gave all the illegal venison to his three companions. In those days, we settled most of our cases by a field acknowledgement of guilt—a legal document where poachers could sign off on the charges against them and pay a fine directly to the game warden. Junior had no problem with this. He paid his two-hundred dollar fine (the maximum back then) in cash, and the case was closed.

There have been many occasions in my career where a tip from an angry or resentful sibling managed to seal a poacher's fate, but this was the only time a family member ever contacted me solely because they were morally opposed to hunting. I was thankful for the call, and wished that it would happen more often.

No sooner had I returned home from Junior Roosevelt's place, than I received another tip regarding a poaching incident. A man who owned a gift shop near the Philadelphia line called to tell me he knew where an illegal deer could be found. I was grateful for the information, but it meant I'd have to turn around and head back toward the city again.

The traffic got heavier as I fought my way south toward Philly. There were long lines at every light, the highways choked with vehicles at each turn. After forty-five minutes and an equal number of traffic lights, I finally arrived at the gift shop.

I stepped inside. A middle-aged man with thinning red hair that fell to his narrow shoulders stepped forward to greet me. He had a pronounced limp and walked with the aid of a sturdy wooden cane. He shook my hand vigorously. "Thank you for coming," he said. "I know the traffic is horrendous this time of day. Hope it wasn't too awful."

"Comes with the territory," I said. "Are you Mr. McCain?"

He smiled amicably. "Shane McCain at your service."

"What can you tell me about the deer?"

"Actually, I'm calling in behalf of a friend. He came into my store just after lunch. Told me he saw a doe hanging in the neighbor's garage next door. Door was open so he walked right in. Said there was a bullet hole in its neck." McCain reached into his pants pocket and pulled out a small envelope. "Deer hair," he said, handing it to me. "I walked over to the garage to see for myself, but the door was closed when I got there. Found the hair on the ground nearby."

"Where can I find your friend?" I asked, taking the envelope from him.

"Oh, he won't get involved any further," said McCain. He turned and stepped behind the counter. "Excuse me, but I have to take some weight off this leg." He eased himself onto a stool and hung his cane on a hook behind him. "Like I said, my friend wants to remain anonymous. That's why I gave you the deer hair. Thought it might help with your investigation."

"Appreciate that," I said. "How about you? Willing to get involved?"

"Absolutely! I have no time for poachers. Just tell me what you want me to do."

"Unless your neighbor admits he has a deer in his garage and invites me in, I'll have to include your name on my affidavit for a search warrant. The deer hair will help, but your name, along with the information you just provided, will be crucial. You okay with that?"

He nodded. "I'm fine with it. Man named Isaiah Smith rents the place. Other than that, I don't know a thing about the guy. He's lived there for about a year. "

I thanked McCain and stepped outside. There was a long driveway that led to Smith's place, a rundown split-level built over a double garage. A roomy chain-link dog pen stood alongside the house. Four husky German Shepherds lined its perimeter and growled menacingly as I approached. They were nasty looking beasts. I stayed clear of them.

There were no vehicles around, but I knocked on the front door anyway, hoping someone would be home. When nobody answered, I got in my patrol car and drove straight to the nearest district court for a search warrant. Because someone had spotted a doe hanging in the garage, I didn't anticipate any difficulty with the judge.

Later that evening, Deputy Bob McConnell and I proceeded to Smith's house armed with the warrant. McConnell was a deputy with the state Fish and Boat Commission, which is funded separately from the Game Commission. Although the natural resources in Pennsylvania are governed by two different agencies, the officers have overlapping powers and often work together. McConnell was a trusted friend, and we frequently teamed up during hunting season.

We were surprised to see that the house looked empty when we pulled in. There were no cars in the driveway, no lights in the windows, nothing. I had timed our arrival for eight o'clock, figuring someone would be home by then. I knocked at the front door but there was no answer, which made me feel pretty uncomfortable. I'd much rather have the suspect be present when I show up with a search warrant in hand. The notion of uniformed officers coming into a home to look for evidence often has a sobering effect on people. More often than not, they'll show you where the illegal stuff can be found rather than have you barge in and search blindly for it. Another problem with an empty house is that we have to find a way inside if no one is around to open up. I don't like the idea of breaking doors down, even though the search warrant gives me that right.

Hoping to buy some time until our suspect showed up, we walked over to the garage and tried lifting the door. To our mutual surprise, it was unlocked and opened easily. But its creaky springs alerted Smith's German shepherds (who evidently were heavy sleepers because they hadn't made a sound until now), and we almost jumped out of our skins as they exploded into a wild fury in the moonless night. They hurled their bodies into the fence, growling savagely. It seemed they wanted to tear us to pieces. One of them yelped in pain as a larger dog turned on it. Then, in a brutal frenzy, the others tore into the hapless creature, one going straight for the neck. Somehow, the dog managed to escape them. Darting into a doghouse, it turned, brandishing a mouthful of pointy teeth as it faced the snarling pack.

"What the—!" cried McConnell.

"Smith's dogs," I shouted over their frenzied barking. "Forgot to mention them!"

We quickly ducked into the garage to get away from them. There was a switch on my right. I flicked it on. Above us, two oversized fluorescent lamps glimmered and flicked before finally lighting up the place. The garage was an easy search. There were no closed storage bins or freezers to inspect. And we could see directly into the open shelves that had been built into the walls on both sides of us. Most were bare, but a few were stuffed with boxes of Christmas decorations, old toys, and other odds and ends. A huge wooden workbench stood at the far end of the garage. Assorted hand tools hung on hooks fastened to the wall above it.

"You'd never know a deer had been in here," said McConnell. "The place is spotless."

"Looks like the floor has been scrubbed with some kind of concrete cleaner," I said. "Wonder if someone got word to him."

McConnell shrugged. "If that's the case, we won't find anything in the house, either."

The notion made my stomach churn. I hated the idea of searching someone's home only to come up empty. The warrant expired at ten o'clock, but I wanted to wait awhile, hoping Isiah Smith would return home. But after an hour passed with no sign of him, we began to search for a spare door key hidden somewhere around the house. We found nothing, and I was about to call off the search when McConnell stepped over to a porch window, pressed his hands flat against the glass, and gently pushed up. It rose effortlessly. He turned and offered a self-satisfied grin. "After you."

I crawled through the unlocked window and slid cautiously into the sterile darkness of Isiah Smith's house, praying that one of his brutal German shepherds wasn't inside. Once on my feet, I groped at the wall until I felt a light switch and flicked it on. There was an upright refrigerator and freezer in the kitchen, so I went directly to it and opened both compartments. Surprised and disappointed to discover it empty, I slipped over to the front door and opened it for McConnell. He stepped inside and we went into the basement hoping to find a chest freezer stocked with venison, but once again, we struck out. Discouraged we hadn't found anything, I decided to end the search. Leaving a copy of the warrant on Smith's kitchen table, we closed up the house and departed.

The following day, I expected a hostile telephone call from Isaiah Smith. After all, his house had been searched in the dark of night while he was away and nothing was found. An innocent man would have been outraged—and rightfully so. Normal behavior would be to scream bloody murder about the injustice that had been done. A demand for an apology for the gross invasion of privacy! The breech of peace! But Isaiah Smith never called, which left absolutely no doubt in my mind, whatsoever, that he was guilty.

I waited another day, just to let him stew a bit, before heading back to Smith's house with Deputy McConnell. Once again, no one came to the door when I knocked, even though a pickup truck was parked in the driveway. We went to the truck and checked its bed, discovering some deer hairs and a faint bloodstain on the floor. We suspected it was from the deer we were looking for, but there was little we could do unless Smith was willing to talk, and so far, we'd been unable to make contact with him. Anticipating a return call, I wedged a business card into Smith's front doorjamb and we left.

My only hope was to get a confession. The man who saw the deer in Smith's garage wouldn't come forth, and a few deer hairs and some dried blood doesn't come close to making a poaching case. So I waited another week, thinking Smith would call, but after hearing nothing from him, Deputy McConnell and I drove to his house once again.

Completely by luck, we pulled into the driveway just as he was walking out the front door. He paused for an instant, and I thought he might duck back inside at the sight of my patrol car. Instead, he closed the door behind him and stepped calmly off the porch to meet us.

A tall and rangy man in his thirties, he had blonde hair cropped short along with a neatly trimmed mustache and beard. He seemed very much at ease, standing there in his driveway—as if he'd been expecting us all along, which of course, he had not.

McConnell and I were in full uniform as we exited my patrol car. "Isaiah Smith?" I called.

He answered with a sheepish smile. "That's right. I knew we'd bump into each other eventually. Guess today's the day."

I stepped close. McConnell at my side. "We're here about the deer you had in your garage. Season's closed, which makes it illegal."

He glanced at his garage door and frowned. "What makes you think I had a deer in there? You searched the place two days ago and didn't find anything."

Attempting to shake him up, I told him something that only someone who saw the deer hanging in his garage could possibly know: "It was a small doe," I said. "With a bullet hole in its neck. Sound familiar?"

No response. His face stone cold. No way was this guy going to choke. I had to fake him out—make him think I had more than I did. Otherwise, we'd get nothing from him.

I took an envelope from my coat pocket and pulled out a tuft of deer hair. Pinching it between my fingers, I held it up. "Someone gave us a souvenir. Said it came from your deer—said they were willing to testify about it in court, too. Is that what you want? A trial. Someone pointing a finger at you?"

Smith stood there and studied me for a moment. Then said, "Who's this witness you're talking about?"

"I won't tell you that. Not yet anyway. I'm here solely to save everyone a day in court: my witness, you, and me. We all have better things to do. Ever hear of a field acknowledgement of guilt?"

"No."

"It's a legal document for people who violate the Game Law. You can plead guilty and avoid court costs by signing one. You pay your fine directly to the Game Commission. Keeps your name out of the newspaper, too."

Smith said nothing, just kept staring at me.

I said, "If we go to court, I'll charge you with the unlawful killing *and possession* of a deer in closed season. But if you settle on a field acknowledgement, I'll go with a single charge of unlawful killing. It cuts the fine in half. Your choice."

"I don't think you can prove anything," he said coolly.

Deputy McConnell said, "Do you think a judge would issue a search warrant if we didn't have a substantial case against you?"

Smith dropped his eyes, lips pressed thin. "How much is the fine if I settle on a field acknowledgement?"

"Two hundred." I gave him a moment, then said, "Look, you think about it. I'll hold up on the paperwork for a few days. You have till the end of the week. After that, it'll be too late."

Driving off, I didn't have a good feeling about our meeting. Smith killed a deer, of that there was no doubt. And he knew I had a witness—how else could I have known his deer was a doe and that it was shot in the neck? But my witness refused to come forth. I never even met the man; only McCain knew who he was, and he refused to get involved any further. We had nothing without a confession, so when two weeks passed without word from Isaiah Smith, I figured it was over unless I could find a way to put more pressure on him. But how? It seemed impossible.

Then, later that week, I got a call from Shane McCain asking about the case.

"It doesn't look good." I said. "Without your friend's testimony about the deer, we don't have a chance."

McCain blew a long sigh into the phone. "No way he'll do that," he declared. "It's his neighbor, and I think Smith suspects him already. Probably why Smith won't admit to anything. He knows he's afraid of him."

"So it's a neighbor, huh?"

"That's right. I didn't tell you before because he's so adamant about not wanting to be involved."

"I understand."

McCain said, "Smith only has two homes bordering him. You saw that when you were there. So he's gotta suspect it was my friend. The other neighbor is his landlord, Herbert Eichmann. Smith rents off him. He knows right well that Eichmann would have confronted him rather than call the game warden. He's an ornery cuss."

"Hmmm. A landlord who's an ornery cuss, you say. That's perfect!"

"What do you mean?"

"I wonder how his landlord would react if I told him about Smith poaching a deer on his property? Could be just what I need to close this case."

"You got a good point there," said McCain. "Look, I got his phone number somewhere. Hold on, I'll get if for you."

I telephoned Eichmann that same day and explained everything to him. He had no idea a deer had been shot on his land, and although he wasn't a hunter, he was especially unappreciative of the fact that it was killed in closed season. "I'll talk to Mr. Smith tonight," Eichmann declared. "Rest assured you'll be getting a call from him by tomorrow morning."

The following day, two months after the investigation began, Isaiah Smith called me to say he wanted to settle on a field acknowledgement of guilt.

I said, "Tomorrow is Saturday, how about meeting me at the state police barracks sometime in the afternoon?"

"Can we do it today?" There was urgency in his voice. "Really. It's gotta be today."

"Sure." I said. "I'll stop by your place in about an hour."

"Thank you, officer. I'll be waiting."

Smith never mentioned that his landlord had contacted him. Instead, he pretended he had evolved into someone with a conscious and said he wanted to get everything off his chest. He told me a small band of deer had been hanging out behind his house every night, so one evening he popped open a window and shot a doe in the neck with his .357 magnum revolver. It was a crime of opportunity he said. Something he'd never done before. He said the carcass was in the dog pen with his four German shepherds the night we searched his place. If we would have looked, we would have seen it— or what was left of it.

Considering the stormy nature of Smith's dogs, the likelihood of anyone inspecting their kennel in the dark was nil at best. I wasn't so sure I believed him, and couldn't help but wonder how many other deer he'd shot illegally over the years. Still, I was glad the case had come to a successful conclusion.

Had it not been for the help of everyday citizens who were willing to get involved and contact the Game Commission, both Junior Roosevelt and Isaiah Smith would never have been brought to justice. Pennsylvania's game wardens are but a thin green line, a mere fraction of officers compared to other police agencies. Without the eyes and ears of the public to help us, many poachers would never be apprehended.

Most wildlife agencies have toll-free poacher hotlines. If you see illegal hunting activity, don't leave it up to someone else to make the call, contact your state game department immediately. Wild birds and animals can't speak for themselves. It's up to you to be their voice in the wilderness.

# Lost Boys

WHEN HEADLIGHTS APPROACHED, the teenaged poachers dropped flat in the field and waited for the car to pass. It was three in the morning on a cold December night.

"They're slowing down!" breathed Derek.

Jackson raised his head and peered through the grass with unease as the vehicle came to a stop beside the '95 Chevy Corsica he'd left by the road.

"That's my mom's car, and I don't want anybody messing with it!" he hissed.

Derek stared in disbelief as Jackson gathered himself into a sprinter's crouch and prepared to charge headlong toward the intruders.

"Wait!" snapped Derek. "It could be the game warden!"

Jackson shook his head, eyes focused dead ahead. "We drove past his house on the way out here. You saw his car parked in the driveway. It ain't the game warden, Derek!"

"But what if it's the cops!—"

But the words came too late, for Jackson had already disappeared into the dark surround. He ran in a blind panic across the frozen grass, his legs battering the ground like pistons in a racing engine.

His eyes were fixated on the stranger's car. He watched the dome light flick on as the occupants exited from separate doors, their human forms mere silhouettes under a pregnant moon. He watched them move to his mother's car, flashlights peering into the windows. Jackson may have been small in stature, but he would take them both on if necessary. Certain they were thieves, he hated them, his anger propelling him at an astonishing gait.

Soon he was on top of them, running full tilt. "Get away!" He shouted. "Get away from that car!"

State Troopers Paul Wolfe and John Garrett straightened to peek over the Chevy's roof as Jackson charged out of the field at them. "State Police!" they called. "Stop!"

The blood in Jackson's veins turned to ice. He glanced at their car, an emergency lightbar on its roof.

*What if it's the cops!*

His expression suddenly changed from one of frenzied anger to a look of comic revelation as he tried to stop, but his momentum was too great, and he went flailing mercilessly into the rear of the trooper's cruiser.

*"Woof!"*

Jackson doubled over in pain, then dropped to the ground like a puppet with its strings cut.

Trooper Wolfe gritted his teeth to suppress a laugh as he stepped around the Chevy. "Hey son, what are you doing out here in the middle of nowhere?" The area was a hotspot for grazing deer and he suspected the young man was poaching.

Jackson lay on the ground, curled into a fetal position, his face knotted into an ugly grimace. "*Argh!* I'm hurtin' man. I think I busted my privates!"

The trooper shook his head pathetically. "What are you, maybe sixteen? You'll be fine, kid. Now get on your feet and quit your bellyaching."

Jackson stared up at him. The troopers palm was placed firmly on the butt of his revolver. "Ow!" pleaded Jackson in an attempt to stall. "I think I might need an ambulance, man."

"Get up and start talking, son! What were you doing back in that field? You been shining deer? Poaching?"

The troopers had observed a spotlight plugged into a cigarette lighter in Jackson's car. The engine was still warm, indicating the Chevy hadn't been there very long. Both officers were hunters. They had little doubt about what he'd been doing.

Jackson couldn't believe his rotten luck. This poaching episode was all Derek's idea in the first place, and he was nowhere in sight. He raised a hand toward the troopers. "Help me up."

"You're kidding," scoffed Wolfe. "You aren't hurt! Scared maybe, but not hurt. Now get to your feet, mister!"

Jackson stood, shoulders hunched inward, fists stuffed protectively over his groin. He looked back into the field, hoping Derek would show.

*But what good would it do?* he thought. *And why should he? So he can get busted too?*

Jackson concentrated, trying desperately to come up with a story about why he was out here, but nothing came to him, nothing even the dumbest cop would swallow.

Trooper Wolfe narrowed his thick brow, his eyes boring into Jackson. "You better start talking young man or you'll be heading for the barracks in cuffs. You've been out shooting deer tonight, haven't you?"

His mind raced. What could he say to throw him off? Then, from out of nowhere, it came to him:

"I wasn't hunting!" he declared. "Honest! I was just cutting across the field toward my girlfriend's house."

Trooper Wolfe grinned in mock sarcasm. "Right. And I'm Santa Claus." He gestured toward Trooper Garrett, a good six-foot-six without shoes. "And this is one of my helpers. He's kind of tall for an elf, don't you think?"

"We're looking for Rudolph," scoffed Garrett. "Have you seen him tonight?"

Jackson looked away and slowly shook his head.

"Do you have any guns in the car?" demanded Wolfe.

"Why would I have guns in the car?"

The trooper stepped into Jackson' face. "Don't play games with me, kid. I grew up around here. There's nothing but woods on the other side of that field, with no houses for another mile or so." He shined his flashlight on Jackson' fists. "Open your hands."

Jackson hesitated.

"Open them or I'll do it for you."

Jackson envisioned the trooper cracking his knuckles with his flashlight and cringed. He was in enough pain already.

Shaking his head with regret, he slowly splayed his fingers, turning his palms upward.

"Blood," remarked the trooper. "Just as I suspected. Tell you what: you want us to believe you were at your girlfriends? Fine! We'll book you on suspicion of murder."

"Murder!" yelped Jackson.

The trooper pulled out a gleaming pair of handcuffs. "If it ain't deer blood then we can only assume it's human. You're coming with us."

"Wait!" gasped Jackson. "I don't even *have* a girlfriend! Derek made me do it. Honest!"

"Do what, kid? Start talking."

Jackson fished a key from his pocket and handed it to the trooper. "Go ahead; open the trunk. The gun's inside. It ain't even mine. It belongs to Derek."

Trooper Wolfe took the key from Jackson and opened the trunk. Reaching down, he grabbed a loaded thirty-caliber rifle and put the breech to his nose. It had been freshly fired.

While he did this, Trooper Garrett walked into the field with his flashlight to look around. He didn't go far before spotting a heavy blood trail.

"Hey Santa," he shouted back at his partner, "I got bad news: looks like Rudolph won't be guiding our sleigh tonight."

Derek could have reached out and touched him. Well, maybe not quite, but he was close enough to hear the grass whisper against his trousers as he passed. He had crawled on his belly a good hundred yards so he could hear them talking when one of the cops broke away and started heading toward the field. Derek flattened himself in the dark, his heart pounding wildly in his chest as the trooper moved toward him. Had he not been eyeballing the blood trail with his flashlight, he would have spotted him for sure.

Jackson was a fool. If he hadn't taken off—and run right smack into the cops for crying out loud!—they'd be down the road with the deer in the trunk already. He should have listened. Stayed put. But he was too high strung. And he was a rank amateur. Bringing him along had been a mistake, but Jackson had a car, and Derek needed one.

Derek wrecked his own car a month ago when, after polishing off a half-case of beer, he veered off the road and rolled down a twenty-foot embankment before slamming into a tree. Lucky thing, that tree, or he would've kept on rolling right into the Susquehanna River. As a result, Derek had walked away with only a few bruises.

He lay motionless in the grass as the trooper continued following the blood trail with his flashlight, its yellow beam steadily fading as he distanced himself. He thought about running. He was fast. Faster than Jackson. Faster than the cops. But lying on the cold ground for so long had caused his joints to grow stiff. His feet were numb, his legs cement. Besides, cops had guns. What if they started shooing? No way could he outrun a bullet!

Now, suddenly, the cop was coming back! His flashlight bobbing in the dark, boots pounding the earth. Derek spread himself flat, wishing he could magically squirm into the ground and disappear. His heart hammered with dread. The cop was heading in a straight line, right for him. He had to get out of his path! Derek crawled backwards on his belly through the high grass but only went a few yards when he had to stop moving or he'd be spotted for sure. He lay flat on the ground, hoping his drab clothing would conceal him in the dark. He could hear the trooper coming, the thump of his boots as he neared, his labored breathing. He risked a fleeting upward glance. The cop passed within inches, but his eyes were locked on this partner by the road and he never looked down.

Derek blew a ragged sigh of relief as he watched the trooper move from the field into the street. He strode directly to Jackson. Got in his face. Derek could hear him, his voice booming like thunder in the night. "There's a dead deer back there, son." He roared. "Do you know what the fine is for poaching? You should be home in bed, not out here taking potshots at deer!" He opened a leather case on his belt and pulled out his handcuffs. Jackson yelped like a whipped puppy when the trooper hooked him up. He took him by the arm and escorted him to the rear of his cruiser, guiding him into the back seat with his free hand on Jackson's head. Then he shut the door.

The other trooper opened the cruiser's trunk and placed the rifle inside. "Any sign of the other guy?" he asked.

"Nope! Just the deer. Nice eight-pointer. Too bad."

Trooper Wolfe closed the trunk and walked around to the driver's door. He was about to get in when he turned and looked back toward the field.

Derek ducked instinctively.

"See something?" asked Garrett.

"Nah! Just got a creepy feeling for a moment. Like we were being watched."

"There's nothing out there but a dead deer. C'mon. This is the game warden's gig anyway. Let's get this kid to the barracks and give him a call."

Derek watched until their taillights disappeared before he stood. He was underdressed for the cold, his limbs deadened from lying on frozen ground. He hopped on the balls of his feet, slapping his arms and legs with his hands to get the blood circulating. It was a long walk back but he had no choice. Jackson was gone, and with him the keys to his mother's car.

He turned and started through the field, intending to zigzag cross-country to his home, when headlights appeared on the road once more. He heard the sound of a powerful engine—a souped-up engine—and knew it wasn't the cops coming back. He thought about running out to the road and flagging them down, perhaps hitching a ride, but something told him to stay put, that trouble was coming.

Derek crouched in the grass and watched as they rounded a bend and began to materialize through the gloom. There was something about the sound of the vehicle that made his blood freeze. Its throaty rumble seemed to be growling at him, telling him to stay away. Then he saw it. An old Ford pickup, its headlights glaring through the Chevy's rear window. The frame set high on its wheels, jacked up with oversized springs, its harsh engine falling into a lumpy idle as the truck came to a stop behind Jackson's car.

The engine shut down. The lights went dead. Two men climbed out.

Both appeared to be in their twenties, each with a can in his hand. They walked to the driver's window and peered inside. "Empty!" said the one. He let out raucous belch that sounded like vomit. "There's a spotlight on the seat. Plugged in, too."

"Think he's out there somewhere?" asked the other.

"Dunno." He turned and cupped a hand at the side of his mouth. "HELLOWWWWWW! ANYBODY OUT THERE?"

Derek remained motionless. Part of him wanted to jump up, announce himself, and beg for a ride. He was freezing. Dreading the long walk home. But he knew better and stayed low.

He watched the man guzzle down his can and pitch in into the field. Wiping his mouth with his coat sleeve, he turned to his partner. "Nope! Guess nobody's home!" Then, to Derek's astonishment, he strolled over to the driver's door and rammed a vicious elbow through the window, sending shattered glass flying into the interior. He reached inside, unlocked the door and jumped in. By the dome light, Derek watched the man's silhouette as he as he rummaged through the vehicle, tossing papers and odd junk over his shoulder as he searched. He was fast. Out within seconds. The trunk conveniently opened from an interior latch as he exited. A quick look told him all he needed to know.

"Nothing!" he barked. "Man, what a waste!"

"Let's get outa here," hooted his partner. "They might come back."

Derek watched the men climb back into the truck and drive off. He waited, shivering from the cold, until the note of its powerful engine finally evaporated into the night. He stood, brushed himself off, and hustled over to the Chevy. He spotted a heavy woolen shawl lying in the open trunk. Jackson's mother must have left it behind. But it was pink, which made him hesitate as he reached for it. He looked over his shoulder as if someone might be watching, then chuckled to himself. Who, the man in the moon? Derek took the shawl and threw it over his shoulders, glad for what little warmth it would provide. Then he closed the trunk and started back across the dark and lonely field toward home.

$W$hen the phone rang, I bolted upright in my bed and stared bleary-eyed at the alarm clock. It was four o'clock in the morning. I'd been in a light sleep, subconsciously waiting for the phone to ring, as it had almost nightly for the past several weeks. Hunting season had me working sixteen-hour days. Sleep was both precious and rare lately. Exhausted, I groped for the receiver on an adjacent night table and put it to my face. "Game Commission," I muttered in semi-consciousness.

"Bill, it's Trooper Wolfe down at the barracks. Sorry to wake you, but we picked up a poacher tonight. A kid. We found a dead buck out in the field that he and another guy killed. He's ready to talk. We have him here at the barracks if you want to see him."

"Definitely," I said. "Give me a few minutes to get into a uniform and I'll be right over."

"Take your time," replied the trooper. "He ain't going anywhere."

A half hour later, I stepped into the State Police Barracks lobby and was greeted by the nightshift dispatcher. He was sitting behind a bulletproof window pecking away on a computer keyboard. He offered a smile of acknowledgment followed by a look that said *I'm too busy to talk*, then motioned me inside with a nod. I walked toward a heavy door that led into the core of the barracks. A buzzer went off, indicating its lock had retracted. I turned the doorknob and stepped into a long, narrow hallway.

From a room to my left, Trooper Wolfe stepped out to greet me. "Bill!" he boomed, his face lighting up. "Thanks for coming. Sorry to drag you out here in the middle of the night."

"No problem," I said. "It'll be daylight soon anyway."

"We caught the kid red-handed," he said. "Killed a nice buck. Shame, too. It would've made a nice trophy for somebody."

"Local?" I asked. It was deer season, and the county was overrun with hunters from out of state and other places throughout Pennsylvania.

"Yeah. He's local all right. He's a talker too. Says he was with a kid named Derek when they shot the deer." Trooper Wolfe filled me in on the details, and then motioned me on down the hall with a sweep of his arm. "He's in the Interrogation Room waiting for you. Be my guest, he's all yours."

J ackson was sitting in a chair, chin down, arms across his boney chest, looking like he just found out he had terminal cancer when I walked into the Interrogation Room. I closed the door behind me, pulled back a chair from the small desk that separated us, and sat down. The room, Spartan by design, contained four white walls with a one-way mirror to our right. Under Jackson's chair lay a short length of heavy chain bolted to the floor for shackling dangerous or unruly prisoners. Jackson eyed it nervously as I pulled a pen and notepad from my pocket. "I understand you were doing some hunting earlier this morning," I said.

"Yes, sir."

"Troopers found one deer. How many others did you kill?"

"We only shot the one. Honest. There was a bunch of 'em in the field, but they disappeared real quick after the first shot."

"We...?"

"Me and Derek."

"Tell me about him."

"I know him from school. That's all. We're not actually friends or anything like that."

I scribbled some information in my notepad and nodded supportively. "Go on."

"He's like this cool dude in school. Chicks dig him, lots of friends, talks the talk and all that—know what I mean?"

"Sure do."

"Well, he comes up to me at lunch break yesterday and starts talking to me, real friendly like. Only he never even looked at me before, and we've been in the same school together since seventh grade." Jackson paused and looked at me, his eyes betraying a sense of remorse. "I knew he was trouble. And I should've just walked away. But other kids in the cafeteria were watching. It made me feel important—him talking to me like that. He said he saw me driving into school, not taking the bus this week. Said he knew where a nice buck was hanging out. Said he aimed to shoot it and asked if I wanted to go with him." Jackson leaned toward me, fingers splayed against the desktop. "I couldn't turn him down, man. I wanted to be his friend. Hang out with him. So I said I'd do it." He shook his head with regret. "Now look where it got me!"

I nodded reflectively. I well-remembered the pressures of my own teenage years in high school: the bullies who went looking for someone to beat up every day, the jocks and cool dudes who got all the attention, the girls who wouldn't give you a second look if you didn't fit into their perspective of coolness. I felt sorry for Jackson. Unfortunately, I'd seen this same situation far too often when dealing with juvenile poachers.

"Tell me what happened tonight," I said.

Jackson dropped his eyes. "My mom doesn't even know I have her car. I snuck out after she went to bed and drove to Derek's house. He came out with a spotlight in one hand and a rifle in the other. He told me to open the trunk so he could hide the gun in case we got stopped. Then he got in the car with the light and we drove past the game warden's house to see if his patrol car was there. It was, which made Derek laugh." Jackson paused and looked at me. "A house on Dogwood Drive. Yours?"

The hairs on back of my neck pricked at the thought of two night-shooters scoping out my house before committing their deed. But there wasn't anything I could do about it. Wyoming County is rural. Everybody was a hunter, or so it seemed; hence, the game warden had near celebrity status. People knew where you lived, who your wife and children were, where you went to church, bought your cars, shopped for clothes, and whether your kids made the honor roll. I ignored his question. "Keep talking."

Jackson nodded, his eyes displaying regret for asking about my house. He said, "We drove to Mehoopany and turned off on some dirt road where Derek said we'd see a nice buck. Don't know the name of it."

"Foxtail Road," I said. "The troopers told me."

Jackson rolled his eyes. "Guess they told you how I ran out of the field and right into their arms too."

"Sure did. Who shot the deer, you or Derek?"

"Derek did. He was shining the light while I drove, but when we saw the buck, he quick turned it off and told me to pull over. I popped the trunk open from the inside so he could get his gun, then he handed me the light. He opened the door real careful, just enough to squeeze out, and snuck back for the rifle. I kept the spotlight on the deer. It was a beauty. Didn't take long before I heard Derek work the action on his rifle. He fired once. The deer was hit solid but it still took to running. Went a good hundred yards before it dropped."

"Then what happened?"

"Derek put the gun back in the trunk and we ran into the field and found the deer. It was still breathing so Derek slit its throat. I watched it twitch for a minute until it stopped moving. Then Derek gutted it out. We were dragging it back to the car when we saw headlights coming, so we ducked down. When the car stopped by my mom's Chevy, I thought they was up to no good and...well, I guess you know what happened next."

I reached into my coat pocket, pulled out a blank sheet of paper, and slid it across the desk along with a pen. "Mind putting all that in writing for me?"

Jackson looked at me, his mouth drawing into a frown while he thought for a moment. "Guess not," he said finally. "I got nothing to hide, and I ain't gonna lie about what we done."

I waited until Jackson finished writing and then had him sign and date the confession. Jackson was a juvenile, and since there was no parent with him, I couldn't use anything he said in court, but a written confession tends to bring closure for some folks, helps finalize things. And although I couldn't present it to a judge, I could show it to his mother, which could prove much more valuable in the end.

"Where I can find Derek?" I asked, tucking the paper back into my coat.

"He lives with his mom. I guess he's home by now; he doesn't have any place else to go."

"Good. Then you can show me where he lives." I stood from my chair. "Let's go."

Derek lived in a rundown singlewide trailer situated along a seldom-used back road in Lemon Township. There was a dim yellow glow coming from a front window, suggesting someone might be awake inside. It was still dark as I pulled to the berm and shut down my engine. I sat for a moment, watching the trailer for any dogs that might be lurking, then turned to Jackson. "Wait here. I shouldn't be long."

Jackson nodded somberly. He looked like he was about to cry. On our way to Derek's, we had stopped to retrieve the buck they'd killed. Jackson howled in pain when he saw his mother's car. I felt bad for the kid, but it could have been worse. Nothing was stolen, and a broken window can always be replaced. I figured Jackson was in for a lot more trouble from his mother than from me, even though the fine he faced for poaching was pretty high.

I cracked open my door and glanced back at him. "It isn't the end of the world, son," I said. "Hopefully you'll learn something from all this." Then I stepped into the cold morning air and closed the door behind me. As I walked toward the trailer, I hoped that one day Jackson would look at this incident as a turning point in his life and be more careful about who he associated with.

Derek's singlewide rested on a half-acre of weedy lawn a good hundred feet uphill from the road. I walked up the gravel driveway to the trailer and followed a worn path in the lawn leading to the front door. I knocked. Soon there came the muffled thump of footsteps. A rotund, middle-aged woman opened the door and stared open-mouthed at my uniform.

"State Game Warden, Ma'am," I said. "Is Derek here?"

Her eyes fluttered at the mention of his name. She nodded, the sagging flesh jiggling on her cheeks. "He's in bed."

"May I come in?" I asked. "I'd like to talk to him."

"But he's sleeping!"

"Then I think you need to wake him up."

She moved back from the door. "What's this all about, officer?"

I stepped inside and closed the door behind me.

"Are you his mother?" I asked.

"Yes. Now please tell me what's going on."

"I'm afraid your son has gotten himself into some trouble," I said. "He was involved in a poaching incident at around three o'clock this morning—"

"But that's impossible!" she said. "He's been right here! Sound asleep all night!"

"Not according to his friend Jackson. He's sitting out there in my patrol car right now. The state police caught him with an illegally killed buck this morning. He claims he stopped here to pick up Derek on his way. Says Derek shot the deer while he held a spotlight on it."

She swallowed hard and shook her head, her face lined with worry. "Is he going to jail?"

"No ma'am. At least not right now. I just want to talk to him."

She nodded toward a doorway to her left. "That's his bedroom. You're welcome to go in there and wake him. He's over eighteen and he'll just have to deal with it on his own. I know *I* don't have the money to pay his fines."

"I'd like you to accompany me," I said. "It's your house. Do you mind?"

She walked to the bedroom and thumped on the hollow wooden door with the curled joint of an index finger. When no one answered, she rapped on it again, her face falling into an angry scowl. "Derek! There's someone here to see you!"

Again, no reply, and I was beginning to wonder if he was home, when his mother pushed open the door and signaled me in with a quick side nod. I brushed past her with attentive caution, my eyes scanning the room for anyone who might be hiding in wait. Asleep uncovered on a rumpled bed, lay Derek. His scrawny, shirtless body heavily inked with some serious body art. He wore his hair long and had a looped, gold-plated earring in his left ear.

"State Game Commission!" I barked. "Wake up!"

Derek, struggling with sleep, slowly propped himself on an elbow and forced open an eye. "Who...?"

"I want to talk to you about the deer you shot."

Derek blinked repeatedly, his brain attempting to focus on the ugly realization that a game warden was standing in his bedroom staring down at him. "Deer...? What are you talking about, man?"

"Don't play dumb with me. You know exactly what I'm talking about."

"Whoa! Wait a minute, man. I was here all night. I don't know nothin' about no deer!"

"That's not what Jackson tells me." I nodded at a pair of jeans and a plaid shirt lying on the floor. "Yours?"

Derek stared at me tortoise-like. "Huh?"

I picked up the jeans. A knife was attached to the belt in a leather sheath. I extracted it, the blade covered with fresh blood and strands of deer hair. "You still want me to believe you didn't kill a deer?"

Derek swung two naked, hairy legs to the floor and sat on the edge of the bed in his underpants. He blew a long sigh and looked over my shoulder at his mother who was standing in the doorway behind me. "Sorry Mom," he said. "He's right. I killed a deer last night."

I told Derek to get dressed and then had him step into the kitchen with me where I handed him a paper and pen and asked for a written confession. He complied, sitting at the kitchen table where he wrote down everything he and Jackson had done from the time Jackson picked him up to his long walk home in the cold. When he was finished, he handed me the pen and paper and said, "How much is my fine gonna be?"

"Eight hundred," I said, tucking his confession in my coat pocket. His mother gasped when she heard this.

Derek held out two hands and shrugged. "I ain't got that kind of money, warden. Might as well cuff me and cart me off to jail right now."

"You'll get your citations in the mail. When you do, call the judge and ask for time payments. She's usually pretty good about it."

Derek pointed an index finger in the air and waggled it. "I'll do that, officer. You're too kind!"

"Don't cop an attitude with me, son!" I said. "You have nobody to blame but yourself."

"That's right," his mother cautioned him. "You hush your smart mouth this instant!"

Derek dropped his eyes and looked away from her.

I left them there. Taking Derek's hunting knife with me, I walked out the door. I still had to get Jackson back to his mother's Chevy.

When I parked next to it, Jackson looked at the smashed window and refused to get out of my car. Instead, he sat with his head bowed, wringing his wrists and squirming in his seat. "She's gonna kill me," he murmured.

"Want me to follow you home? Talk to her? I can tell her that you cooperated with me. That might soften her a little."

Jackson looked up and shook his head. "She'd be too embarrassed if your car was parked at our house. The neighbors would gossip. It'd just make things worse."

"Okay." I said.

"I appreciate you offering, though."

He was shaking.

"Jackson?"

"Yeah?"

"You're going to get through this," I said. "It won't be easy, but you'll get through it. Your mother loves you and she'll forgive you. Maybe not at first, but she will."

"I hope so," he said bleakly.

"I want you to try something for me," I said.

"What's that?"

"Take a deep breath through your mouth—deep as you can, and exhale slowly through your nose. It's something I do when I'm troubled. It helps me relax."

He looked at me with uncertainty for a moment, then turned and filled his chest with air. I watched as he expelled a long, slow breath out through his nose.

"Again," I said.

He took another lungful, holding it awhile before releasing.

"Once more," I encouraged.

He did. And he began to grow calm.

"Whenever you're scared, I want you to do that until you feel better. Okay?"

"Yessir," he said, a faint shadow of relief crossing his face.

"Good. Time to go."

Jackson took another deep breath and exhaled slowly through his nose. Then he opened the door and stepped out.

Hoping the best for him, I waited until he started the Chevy and drove off before dropping my Bronco into gear. The eastern sky had brightened. My day was just beginning.

# Dazed and Confused

THE TWO DEER HUNTERS to my left were in a field about seventy yards away, watching my marked Ford Bronco as I cruised down the dirt road bordering their farm.

I continued driving, keeping them in sight, when I came upon a truck parked along the road. Two men sat inside. I had cited them the day before for an untagged deer, so I pulled behind and got out for a chat. As I walked toward their pickup, I kept a wary eye on the hunters to my left.

"Any luck today?" I said, approaching the driver's open window.

"Nope! Didn't see a thing." He nodded toward the hunters in the distant field. "But they got one a few minutes ago. Looks like they're having all the luck today."

I glanced over at the hunters. "A doe, I hope."

"Dunno." He turned toward the passenger. "Did you see any horns, Jerry?"

"I couldn't see what it was. All I know is the tall guy fired three quick shots, then they both started whooping and hollering real excited like." He looked over my shoulder at them and chuckled perceptively. "They were kneeling by the carcass, gutting it out, when they spotted your car. Now they're standing there, watching you like a hawk, man. They gotta be up to no good."

I thanked them and walked back to my patrol car. Sitting behind the wheel, I could see the two men in the field clearly. They stood facing each other in conversation.

I recalled the day I first ran across them. It was several years earlier, during a hot July afternoon, when I received an anonymous tip about two men shooting randomly at deer from their vehicle. I drove to the area where they'd been spotted and stopped a suspicious car. I had the occupants step out of the vehicle so I could search it. They were father and son, the kid maybe sixteen at the time. As I questioned them about the incident, a sickly sweet smell, like that of decomposed flesh, suddenly drifted my way. At first, I thought it might be from a roadkilled deer somewhere. But I soon realized the unpleasant aroma came from my suspects. They stood before me in rumpled clothes blotched with brown filth, looking like they hadn't bathed in months. Dad had half his teeth rotted out of his head. Junior still had his choppers, but his gums were encrusted with a heavy black substance that might have been chewing tobacco. If not, then perhaps some wretched gum disease. Dad smiled at me when I asked about the rifle in the front seat. They were woodchuck hunting, he said. I was welcome to check the rifle; it was unloaded, nice and safe, he assured me.

I looked at the kid, eyes dark and vacant. "Woodchuck hunting, huh?" I said.

He grinned mockingly and nodded at me. Like father like son, I figured.

They were the Dungs. Redman and his son, Ricky Lee. I continued to get sporadic reports about their illegal hunting activity over the years since that day but never managed to catch up to them.

It looked like this might be the day.

I cranked the ignition and started down the road until my vehicle was parallel with them. Both continued to watch as I pulled to the weedy berm and exited. I only took a few steps when Redman turned away, his fat legs quickly propelling him into the surrounding woods.

Ricky Lee stood watching me, a good fifty yards out, as I waded toward him through the heavy brush. He had a deer down for sure. Had to, or he would have run just like his father.

As I came closer, I saw his arms were covered with blood up to his elbows. A dead deer lay partially obscured in the tall weeds behind him. He'd just finished gutting it.

"Looks like you got one," I said.

"Yep," he replied, wiping sweat from his forehead with the back of a bloody hand. "A nice, fat one!"

Playing dumb, I asked, "Who was with you before?"

"My pop."

"Why'd he take off like that?"

Ricky Lee grinned cunningly, his slick, blackened gums making my stomach flutter. "Pop had to use the outhouse," he said. "Go and see for yourself if you want."

"My business is with you right now. I want to see your hunting license."

He turned. Pinned to the back of his jacket was a plastic license holder. The viewing window displayed his 1989 hunting license. I pulled the cardboard license from the holder and checked to make sure it wasn't his father's. It was Ricky Lee's.

The boy had grown since I saw him last. He was in his late teens now and taller than his dad. He had an angular jawline with a broad forehead and raven shoulder-length hair. His eyes were dark and empty. When you looked into them, you saw only two dead coals.

I handed his license back and sidestepped him for a closer look at the deer. Ricky Lee's coolness led me to believe I'd find a legal doe, so I was surprised to see a healthy set of antlers protruding from its head. Here he was, standing in the presence of a state game warden while covered in blood with an illegal deer at his feet. Yet he seemed not to care, as if we were merely high school classmates having a casual discussion about homework.

"This is a buck!" I said to him.

Ricky Lee looked at me with open indifference and said, "I know."

"Look," I began patiently, "this is a four-point buck. Buck season is over. It is now doe season...."

He looked at me with an expression of uncomprehending curiosity. I was surprised he didn't have a built-in alibi like so many others: *I didn't see any horns! I shot at a doe and hit this one by mistake! I just found it here!* Or, my favorite of all: *Deer? What deer?*

Something. Anything!

But this man simply gazed at me as if the idea of seasons and bag limits was something he'd never heard before.

"You have an illegal deer," I pressed. "A buck. Want to tell me why?"

He looked down at the deer as if to verify that antlers were indeed growing from its skull, then shrugged indifferently. "I saw a deer, so I took a shot."

"It didn't matter that it wasn't buck season?" I said. "You hit it in the head." You had to see its antlers!"

"They run too fast," he said. "You'll never get one if you take the time to look!"

His Remington rifle was lying across the deer's rump. I picked it up and opened the action. Ejecting the magazine, I dropped it into my coat pocket and checked the Weaver scope mounted on the receiver. It was on 8-power.

I held onto the rifle and said, "How far away was the buck when you shot it?"

"About seventy yards."

"At that distance the antlers should have looked like a hat rack! Besides, the idea isn't to shoot first and then go see what you hit."

There was a shadow of movement to my right. I turned quickly. Redman was hoofing it toward me. Short, squat, and bandy-legged, he called out, "Hey, what's all the commotion about?"

Unlike his son, Redman hadn't changed at all. He wore a loose pair of ragged jeans cinched up with a length of rope under his protruding gut. His orange vest, intended to be seen from afar, was streaked with so much grime that it had become almost useless as a safeguard from careless hunters. He waddled toward us in a breathless huff, his vest unzipped and open over his bulging abdomen, his unkempt hair jutting in greasy tufts below a grubby ball cap.

"Wasserman, right?" he puffed, thrusting out a hand.

*Pop had to use the outhouse…*

86

"We have an illegal deer here," I said, ignoring his outstretched palm.

Redman glanced at his son's kill and frowned. "Illegal!" he remarked, dropping his hand. "It's deer season, ain't it?"

"*Doe* season," I said.

Redman took a second look at the deer. "Well I'll be! It's got horns!"

"You didn't know that when you ran off before?"

Redman shook his head vehemently. "No sir! I never saw horns. Its head was in the bushes, just like it is now, when I got this awful pain in my belly and had to run to the outhouse. Something I ate!" His eyes widened suddenly. "Uh-oh!" he groaned. His body suddenly stiffened, face twisting into a painful grimace, teeth black and broken. "Ohhhh!"—

There came a long staccato burst that sounded like his jeans were being ripped apart at the seams. Redman sighed with relief, then quickly offered a sheepish smile, aware that I was downwind, a few feet away. "Sorry, warden," he said, clutching his stomach. Fried squirrel and beans last night. Never again!"

I nodded stiffly. All I wanted to do was get back in my car, away from these Neanderthals, but I couldn't. I was certain Redman knew that his son had killed an illegal deer; but it would be impossible to prove in court, so I decided to switch gears and question him about the complaints I'd received over the past several years.

"I've been getting calls about semi-automatic rifle fire coming from your property, especially after dark," I said. "Want to tell me what's going on?"

Redman shrugged. "No idea. I've been hearing the shots too, but they're not coming from me." He squinted and scratched at his unshaven face. "You know, some folks around here don't like me much. Never could figure out what for. I suspect that's why they're accusing me, though."

I hadn't expected a confession. I just wanted him to know that I was aware of it, hoping it might curtail the shooting and save some wildlife when I told him. In truth, I'd heard the shooting myself in the wee hours of the morning while posted on a hill overlooking Dung's fifty-acre farm (or what used to be one, anyway. He hadn't grown anything but weeds on the property in decades.). It was rapid fire that could only have come from a semi-auto. A quick burst of ten shots, maybe more. I suspected he was shooting at a deer from his back yard. There were no lights to give away his position, and from my station, several hundred yards away, it was impossible to pinpoint exactly where it was coming from. By the time I'd get my vehicle started, it would be over. And a quick jaunt downhill without headlights revealed nothing.

"I'll have deputies working this area more frequently," I said. "We'll catch 'em eventually. We always do."

Redman pressed his hands into his lower abdomen and squeezed his knees together. "Scuze me," he groaned, "but I feel another attack coming on. It's gonna be a bad one."

I didn't know if he was faking it, but I didn't want to find out. Besides, I'd already decided not to prosecute him. His son was eighteen. He alone would be responsible for his illegal kill.

"You better go," I insisted.

Redman pivoted on his heels, running bandy-legged and bent, he high-tailed it back toward the outhouse, his faded orange vest flapping in the wind.

Ricky Lee smiled in admiration, black gums glistening in the morning sun, as he watched him running through the waist-high weeds. The game warden was no match for his wily pop.

I pulled out my note pad and began writing.

"What are you doing?"

"I'm jotting down some information for your citation."

"You mean, like a ticket?"

"That's right."

"What for?"

"Killing a buck in closed season."

Ricky Lee shook his head with disgust. "How much is the fine?"

"Five hundred dollars."

"What!" he gasped. "You gotta be kidding! I don't have that kind of money!"

"Then you'll have to ask the judge for time payments."

"Time payments! This was all a mistake! I didn't know it was a buck!"

"A mistake is when you use poor judgment," I said. "What you did was no mistake—it's called negligence at best. Your deer was an obvious buck; the antlers were impossible to miss considering you had a scope mounted on your rifle."

"I'm taking this to court!" declared Ricky Lee. "This ain't fair!"

"Suit yourself," I said. "The judge's contact information will be on the citation. It'll be in the mail within a week."

"What happens to my deer?"

"I'm confiscating it."

"You mean I can't keep it? It's already dead! What do you have to take if for?"

"We don't let people keep their unlawfully killed game. It's part of the penalty for poaching. Now how 'bout we each take hold of an antler and drag this thing back to my vehicle."

Ricky Lee sneered at me. "I ain't helping you do nothing!" Then he turned and stomped off toward his house.

I left him go and dragged the heavy carcass back to the road alone. I could hear distant shooting all around me. Hunting pressure would be substantial, as it always was during our three-day doe season. So after securing the carcass to my steel big game carrier, I slid back inside my vehicle and resumed my patrol.

I hadn't gone more than a mile when I came upon a pickup truck parked along the road. There was a bloody smudge on the top rim of its tailgate.

I pulled over and walked back for a closer look. Sure enough, two freshly killed does were lying inside the bed.

Both had been gutted, steam drifting lazily from their open bellies as I examined them. Ten yards away, two hunters were kneeling in the woods, licenses in trembling hands as they hurriedly filled out their tags, pretending not to notice me.

I called over to them. "It's too late for that," I said.

They both looked up at me. "Huh?"

"It's too late," I repeated, walking over to them. "That was supposed to be done at the kill site, before you dragged the deer out of the woods."

"But we're filling them out now!" they protested.

"No you're not," I said with an outstretched arm. "Hand them over."

There was no doubt in my mind that they intended to take the two deer home and continue hunting with their unused tags. I'd seen it time and again over the years. And they might have gotten away with it, had I not happened by.

They stood simultaneously, both men handing me their tags with long faces. "We were gonna tag the deer," they complained. "Honest!"

I pocketed the tags and took their hunting licenses so I could copy names and address for their citations. This was one violation that I never gave warnings for. Too many hunters abused the system by intentionally failing to tag their deer. And too many of them were excellent liars when it came to facing a hundred-dollar fine. *I was gonna do it* was their common mantra, and I'd long ago given up trying to figure out who was telling the truth and who wasn't.

I walked back to my patrol car and grabbed a citation pad. Both men stood silently as they watched me write two citations. When I finished, I handed them their copies. "You're getting off easy," I said. "I could confiscate your deer, too."

They looked astounded. "You could take our deer!"

"That's right. You're supposed to fill out your tag and attach it to the deer before transporting your kill. Make sure that's what you do next time."

The hunters folded their citations and stuffed them in their coat pockets. They stared at me in mutual silence as I turned and walked back to my vehicle.

What I didn't tell them is that I almost never confiscated an untagged deer. I handled hundreds of roadkills and illegals each year (over ten thousand throughout my career) and didn't need the hassle. Most of my roadkills were transported to a remote section of the county and dumped into the Deer Pit, a six-foot-deep trench dug by a Game Commission backhoe. On a hot day, you could smell the decaying flesh a half-mile away. Fortunately, vultures, bears, and coyotes didn't seem to mind, and would make short work of the stinking, maggot-infested carcasses.

Illegally killed deer were a different matter. They had to be preserved until their respective cases were adjudicated. These were stored in a Game Commission freezer, which meant I had to haul them back to the main office, affix them with a confiscation tag bearing the name and address of the violator, and drag them into a fifteen-by-fifteen walk-in freezer filled to over-capacity with dead critters from ten different counties within the northeast region of the state. Wrestling a deer, or worse, a bear, into the freezer was challenging at best, as this required dragging the heavy carcass over a huge pile of frozen corpses confiscated by a dozen other game wardens. Because the animals were frozen stiff as rocks, it made footing precarious at best. One misstep might easily cause a tumble, and with all the heavily racked deer lying about, there was a good chance you'd end up with the boney point of an antler jammed into your flesh.

When dealing with untagged deer, it was much easier to keep the tags for evidence rather than take the whole animal. If I thought there might be a hearing, I'd photograph the kill; however, my sworn testimony that a tag was not properly attached was accepted by every judge I ever encountered.

I'd seen all kinds of tagging schemes over the years. Some hunters would be extra sneaky and attach a blank tag to the deer, hoping I wouldn't notice. The plan was to get the deer home and pocket the clean tag so they could go back out and kill another. The more devious schemers would take it a step further by filling in the month and year in the three spaces provided for the date, leaving the middle one for the day blank, which gave them the rest of the month to hunt with the tag. Others would fill out the cardboard tag ever so lightly in pencil, intending to erase the information once they returned home. There were additional tricks, but I'm sure you get the picture by now.

All these scenarios were running through my mind as I slid inside my patrol car and started the engine. I dropped my vehicle into gear and started down the road when my agency radio blurted a message about a violation less than a mile away, the dispatcher informing me that a woman was on the phone complaining about a hunter who had shot a deer too close to her house.

Pennsylvania has a Safety Zone law that prohibits hunting or shooting at wildlife within one hundred and fifty yards of any occupied building unless you have permission from the property owner. Safety Zone violations are one of our most common complaints; unfortunately, many are unwarranted, especially in the more urbanized areas of the state where the mere sight of a hunter sitting in a vehicle parked along the road might be reason enough for folks to call nine-one-one. Wyoming County was rural; consequently, I didn't get many safety zone complaints. But when I did, they were usually justified, and more flagrant violations.

I hit the gas and keyed my mike, telling the dispatcher I had an ETA of ten minutes, hoping to get there in time to catch the hunter still in the act. Once a violator moves out of a safety zone, it becomes more difficult to make a case, often requiring that the complainant appear in court to testify about what they saw, in order to successfully prosecute the case. Most folks don't want that, preferring that the officer handle the violation without their direct involvement.

When I reached the property, I pulled up a long driveway and parked alongside a modest one-story ranch home that sat fifty yards back into a field along a country road. There was no hunter in sight, and as I stepped toward the front door, a woman in her mid-forties came out to meet me.

"Thanks for coming so quickly," she said.

"Is the hunter still on your property?"

She put a hand to her forehead, shielding the low sun from her eyes, and looked out toward the road. "He took off," she said. "But I have a feeling he'll be back."

Her optimistic tone surprised me. "Why do you say that?"

She pointed into the field. "There lies his deer."

Sure enough, a hundred yards away lay a dead doe.

"Did you get a good look at him?"

She shook her head. "Couldn't. He was too far away."

She went on to say that she'd been watching a small band of deer from her kitchen window when a man driving a gray Ford stopped in the road broadside to them. He exited the vehicle with a rifle and leaned over the hood, pointing his gun at the deer. With one shot, he dropped the doe in its tracks, then ran into the field and gutted the animal. Rather than drag the deer out to the road, he walked back to his vehicle and drove it across her field in an attempt to retrieve the carcass. But recent rains had softened the ground, and his Ford began to bog down, so he made a quick, tight circle back to the road, his tires carving a deep furrow into the ground as he vacated the property.

Just as she finished telling me this, we heard a vehicle approaching. "I'll bet that's him right now!" she declared.

We watched a gray Ford Taurus come cruising along the backcountry road and steer onto her front lawn, barely slowing down. The driver never looked our way or he would have seen my car; instead, he remained totally focused on the deer. Choosing a different path this time, he drove across high ground, avoiding the soft, low area by the carcass, where he stopped fifty yards from the deer.

I started walking hurriedly toward the vehicle. The man's back was toward me as he opened the trunk. I expected him to retrieve the deer quickly and take off, but instead he strolled casually to the carcass before kneeling by its side to fill out his big game tag.

*Is the man daft?* I thought. Did he not understand that the gaping ruts from his car were property damage? That he was hunting in an obvious safety zone? That the deer had been shot from the road—illegally? And now he wants to tag it! As if everything were perfectly fine!

He never heard me as I stepped up behind him. "What do you think you're doing?"

The sun was at my back. Startled, he turned and squinted into it, his initial surprise quickly changing to an expression of incomprehension, as if in wonderment as to why a game warden would ask such a silly question.

"I'm filling out my tag," he said. "I shot this deer." He stood slowly, favoring his knees with a grimace. "Is there something wrong?"

"Nobody gave you permission to hunt here," I said. "And you've damaged this field with your car."

He looked at the gouged earth. "Didn't mean to do that. Got out fast as I could once I realized it was soupy."

"Let's see your hunting license."

He handed it to me. His name was Frank Rainwater. He was from a neighboring county. I stuffed the license in my back pocket. "You shot the deer from the road, in a safety zone," I said. "The landowner doesn't appreciate any of that."

"What's a safety zone?" he asked. "I don't see any signs."

"See the house and barn behind me?" I said.

He glanced over my shoulder. "Yes."

"Both buildings are less than a hundred and fifty yards from here." I directed my gaze at his deer. "Your deer was killed in a safety zone. It doesn't have to be posted; as a hunter, it's your responsibility to keep a safe distance from any occupied buildings."

"But how am I supposed to know about a law like that?"

"Read the digest that came with your hunting license," I said. "It's in there—along with all the other game laws you broke today."

Rainwater looked at me for a long moment. "Am I in trouble?"

"I'll be writing a few citations. I want you to wait here while I go back for my vehicle."

I wasn't about to haul his deer any farther than necessary, so I walked to my patrol car and drove it back, parking behind his Ford. Then I lowered my big game carrier and dragged his deer over to it.

"You're not taking my deer, are you?" he asked in astonishment.

"It's an unlawful kill. You don't get to keep it."

"I can't believe this!" he cried. "Doe season's almost over. I might not get a chance to kill another one."

I ignored his whining and piled the deer on top of Ricky Lee Dung's buck, tying them both down with rubber straps. Rainwater stood back and watched, his expression turning as somber as if he were mourning the loss of a friend. When I finished securing the deer, I sat in my patrol car, grabbed my citation pad from the glove box, and wrote him up for five separate game law violations, including one for property damage.

I handed him his copies and watched as he thumbed through the stack, his lips moving in concentrated silence as he mentally calculated the fines at the bottom of each page.

"Fifteen hundred dollars!" he cried. "And you're taking my deer too?"

"You have the right to a hearing."

Rainwater threw up his hands in frustration. "A hearing! Great! Now I have to take time off from work. It's not even worth hunting anymore!"

I stood and watched him get back into his Ford Taurus. He slammed the door and dropped it in gear. Then he backed out the same way he came in, careful to avoid any soft earth. When he hit the road, he threw a spray of cinders behind him as he stormed off.

Later that day I saw him again. Road hunting with a boy.

## Author's Note

Frank Rainwater pled guilty to all five charges and made monthly time payments for a year until his fine was paid in full. In addition, his privileges to hunt and trap in Pennsylvania were revoked for three years.

Ricky Lee Dung requested a hearing in district court and was subsequently found guilty. He was ordered to pay $530 in fines and court costs. His privileges to hunt and trap in Pennsylvania were revoked for one year.

# An Inconvenient Truth

**STEPPING INTO LINE TO PAY** for groceries, Natalie was stunned by what she overheard:

"It was the shot of a lifetime he keeps telling me!" complained the cashier. She was in her early thirties and whined through her nose with a heavy New York accent as she bagged goods for a female shopper. "I had to listen to him blow his horn about it all day long! 'I can't believe I shot an eagle! I can't believe I shot an eagle!'"

"Poor you!" said her customer in a tone dripping with sympathy "Typical man. They all love to talk about themselves, don't they?"

"That's my Ben all right. He'll brag about the eagle until he gets his deer. Which he always does. Then he'll brag about the deer and what a great shot he made. For weeks!" She put the last of several cans into a brown paper bag and smiled wearily. "He left the house at four this morning to go bow hunting. All I need is another trophy hanging on my walls to dust!"

Her customer shook her head as she swiped a credit card. "Well, at least he can't mount the eagle he shot!" she snorted. "That's one trophy he'll have in memory only."

"Thank goodness for that," said the cashier. She lifted the grocery bag from the counter and handed it off. "Have a good one!"

"You too, Zelda."

Natalie made a mental note of the cashier's name. Then, after paying for her items, she left the store and drove directly home. She was relieved to see her husband's Toyota Corolla in the driveway. He was home for lunch as usual. She parked behind him, grabbed her two grocery bags off the seat, and hustled inside.

He was sitting at the kitchen table, eating a turkey sandwich when she walked through the door. He took one look at her and stood. Dropping the sandwich on a plastic dish, he grabbed the bags from her arms and set them on an adjacent counter. They'd been married long enough for him to know something was wrong. "What is it Natalie? Everything okay?"

She told him what she'd overheard, her face lined with concern. "They were talking about it so casually," she said. "As if it were nothing! But it was an eagle, Jerry. That woman's husband shot an eagle!"

"Wow!" I've never even seen one around here before."

"That's because they're an endangered species. It must have just been passing through—fall migration or something."

"That's too bad. Guy's a real jerk!"

She pivoted and grabbed the phone off the wall.

"What are you doing Natalie?"

"I'm reporting it!"

"Whoa, baby whoa! You don't want to do that."

"Jerry. The man shot an eagle. Somebody needs to know about it."

"Relax a minute babe. Let's talk about this."

She hung up and pulled a chair from the table. "Okay," she said, plopping into the chair with a pout. "Let's talk. You first."

Jerry sat across from her, their feet practically touching. "We don't know anything about these people, Nat. I mean, the guy has a gun; he shoots things. What if he comes after us?"

Natalie recoiled at the suggestion. "I won't tell the police my name. No one will ever know it was me."

Jerry offered a gentle smile. "They'll have your number recorded the second you call."

"Then I'll go down to the corner and use a pay phone."

Jerry looked at her. "They're gonna want you to come to the station, give them a written statement. They're gonna want to get a search warrant for his house, which means your name will be on the police records as an informant. You could be subpoenaed to court, too. Do you want that?"

Natalie's expression went from a stony glare of conviction to one of hesitancy and doubt. "You're scaring me, Jerry. Now I don't know what to do."

He took her hand softly into his. "The eagle is already dead. You can't bring it back. We got our own problems, Natalie. You're pregnant, I'm working two jobs, the mortgage is late every month…" He paused and glanced through the kitchen window at his car in the driveway. "And I'm waiting every day for the repo man to show up. C'mon, babe, let it go. We got our own problems to deal with."

Natalie dropped her chin and looked over her forehead at him with puckered lips. "You mad at me?"

"No, I'm not mad at you baby. It's just that you're so…I don't know—principled I guess. Everything's black and white with you. No wiggle room. And that's one of the things I love about you, but—"

Natalie touched his lips with an index finger. "Shhh. It's okay, Jerry. I'll let it go." Then she reached across the table and pulled the plate with his sandwich in front of her.

Her husband reached for it but Natalie was too quick. She swept the sandwich off its plate, jumped from her seat, and scurried around the corner out of sight.

"Hey!" cried Jerry with a smile in his voice. Then he leaped from his chair and chased after her.

More than a month had passed since the incident at the grocery store, and Natalie rarely thought about it any longer. But late one night, as she and her husband were watching television, Natalie began flipping through programs until she unexpectedly came upon the National Geographic Channel airing a documentary on eagles. Natalie stared wide-eyed at the screen as a bald eagle soared through a sapphire sky on broad, flattened wings, the snow-white feathers of its head and tail vivid under a golden sun. *The bald eagle is the national bird symbol of the United States*, the narrator proclaimed. *However, pesticides like DDT wreaked havoc on bald eagles as the chemical was collected in fish, the chief diet of this bird, weakening their eggshells and severely limiting their ability to reproduce.*

Jerry looked over at his wife and knew she was going to bring up the guy who killed the eagle again. He thought about grabbing the remote and changing channels but it was too late. Natalie appeared to be in a hypnotic trance, totally focused on the program as it went on to show two young eaglets in a nest the size of a compact car, their fragile bodies covered with downy, grayish white feathers as two adult birds soared overhead. *Bald eagles are believed to mate for life*, the narrator continued. *During nesting season, both birds protect their nest from predators, and the thirty-five days of incubation duties are shared by the male and the female eagle—*

"*Ohhhh!*" sobbed Natalie. Wet tears streamed down her cheeks. "They're just like us, Jerry. All they want is to be married and have babies." She was well into her second trimester and had become more emotional then he'd ever seen her before.

Jerry flicked off the TV and slid next to her on the couch. Wrapping an arm around her, he pulled her close. "Hey, babe, I didn't know the eagle thing was still bothering you that much."

Natalie snuggled close. "I was starting to forget about it, but now I realize I can't. They mate for life, Jerry! The eagle that man killed had a companion, a mate, and they'll never be together again. Oh, Jerry, that is so terrible. We have to report what happened—what I know. We just have to!"

He placed a curled finger under her chin and lifted her face. Looking into her liquid eyes made his heart melt. "First thing tomorrow morning," he said. "I'll go into work late if I have to. You can make the call. I'll stay home with you until we find someone who can help us."

Natalie was referred to the Pennsylvania Game Commission after calling the state police first. She copied the number on a notepad lying next to the phone and immediately redialed. It rang twice when a female dispatcher picked up. "Game Commission," she said in a voice flat and disciplined.

Natalie swallowed hard. "I...I want to report someone for shooting an eagle."

"Can I have your name, please?"

"I'd rather not tell you that."

There was a pause. "You don't have to, ma'am, but it would help if the officer needs additional information."

"I can't give you my name. I'm calling about a woman who works at the grocery store here—a cashier. Her husband shot an eagle. I heard her talking about it with another customer."

"You're sure about this?"

"Of course I am!"

"When did this happen?"

Natalie counted back mentally for a moment, the phone pressed to her ear. She could hear a radio transmission in the background, an officer responding to a call, his voice tinny and distant: "*Five-three-eight to Dallas, I'm in route...*"

"Ummm, it was about six weeks ago, I guess," she said.

"And you're just reporting it now?"

Natalie winced at the dispatcher's tone. "Better late than never, they say, right?"

"Yes, ma'am. I didn't mean to be critical. I'm going to need the name of the cashier and the location of the grocery store. We'll have an officer come out and investigate the incident. Are you sure you don't want to give me a name or phone number where you can be reached?"

"I'm sorry but I can't do that," insisted Natalie. "This is a small town. Word gets around. Besides, it wouldn't do any good. I'm giving you everything I know right now. Just tell the officer to speak with a woman named Zelda. She works at the Acme in Bellville. She's there every day. Please...promise me you'll to that."

"Don't worry, ma'am, we investigate all calls regarding poaching. Besides, that's Officer Malone's district you're talking about. He's new, but he's one of our hardest working wardens. He'll be there as soon as he can."

Wildlife Conservation Officer Boyd Malone regarded the news of an eagle killing with keen interest. He was disappointed that the information had come so long after the fact, but figured a stale case was better than no case at all. And since deer season had ended, things had slowed down drastically compared to the long days he'd been putting in. He had time to breathe a little now, his daily routine mellowing to the more mundane tasks of removing highway killed deer from state roads and checking up on a few beaver trappers. But Malone liked to be busy, he loved catching poachers; hence, he was downright bored of late. Heavy snows had blanketed the county in a monotonous white powder for months, making foot travel difficult for late season small game hunters and their dogs. He'd spent the last several days patrolling the surrounding countryside without so much as a distant glimpse of a hunter. To help break the tedium, Malone made weekly trips to headquarters to chat with dispatchers and office staff, but you could only drink so much coffee, and after an hour or so, he'd bail, thankful he didn't have to stay inside one of those stuffy cubicles shuffling papers all day long.

He was a recent graduate of the Ross Leffler School of Conservation, better known as the Game Commission Training School, where all new cadets spend twelve grueling months learning about wildlife management, law enforcement, land management, public relations, firearms training, self-defense tactics, and agency administrative procedures. All cadets lived at the school through the week and only got home on weekends. For Malone, it had been a year of hell. He hated being cooped up in class every day.

The prospect of making good on an eagle case had put the bounce back in his step. Winter doldrums, with almost no cases to work, had taken its toll on him. But his emotions ran in two directions at once: while he looked forward to working the case, the news that someone had killed an eagle saddened him. There were no nesting bald eagles nearby, even though a large river bordered the county, and this particular eagle could have been the beginning of a comeback for these regal birds.

Figuring his neighboring officer, Sam Briscoe, was probably just as bored as he was, Malone gave him a call, asking if he'd like to assist with the investigation.

"Does a one-legged duck swim in circles?" said Briscoe. "Is a frog's butt watertight? Does a bear—"

Malone barked a laugh into the phone. Briscoe had recently graduated from the training school along with

Malone and twenty-three other men. Malone had taken a liking to him almost immediately; the fact that they both had a background in the military helped them form a solid bond. Upon graduation, they were assigned neighboring districts in the same county and would often work together on big cases.

"Okay, Sammy, okay! I get it. You free right now? The case is stale and I want to get started on it."

"Bored silly just like you, pal. Tell me what you've got."

"Headquarters said they got a call from a woman who overheard a checkout girl talking about an eagle that her husband shot. It happened more than a month ago, and the informant refused to give her name, but the dispatcher says she sounded pretty sincere. The checkout girl works at the Acme not far from here. Name's Zelda. Figured I'd go down and see if she'll talk."

"Guess that's all you can do. No way a judge will grant a search warrant based on anonymous information." Briscoe paused for a moment, then asked, "Want me to call Harper. See if he wants to tag along."

"Sure," said Malone. "We might need him."

Claude Harper was a United States Fish & Wildlife Agent assigned to eastern Pennsylvania. He was stationed close by, and because eagles were considered an endangered species under Federal law at the time (1993), he agreed to assist with the investigation. The penalty for killing bald or golden eagles varied, but imprisonment and extremely heavy fines were possible.

All heads turned as two uniformed officers strode into the grocery store and approached the store manager. Harper waited outside, thinking it would be overkill to have all three of them converge on a single female suspect. The manager, a short, droopy-eyed, self-professed animal lover in his late fifties, frowned when he learned that one of his employees might be involved in an eagle killing.

"It's not good for business to have two armed officers questioning me like this," he said. "People are staring."

Turning his back, he motioned them to follow him with a pudgy hand.

The wardens trailed him down a long and narrow hallway, walking past two restrooms reserved for customers before entering a small employee's kitchen that led into a twelve-by-twelve room accommodating a wooden desk cluttered with papers and a metal file cabinet. The floor was covered in puke-yellow linoleum, the walls hospital white. A wastepaper basket overflowing with trash and a cheap imitation leather chair were parked behind the manager's desk.

"Would someone bring chairs in from the kitchen?" asked the manager as he took a seat behind his desk. "That way everyone can sit when I call Zelda in." He picked up his phone and dialed out. A muffled voice responded on the other end.

"Have Zelda come to my office immediately," he said.

Briscoe walked out and retrieved three metal folding chairs. He set them in front of the manager's desk but remained standing.

"Coffee, gentlemen?" asked the manager. "It's Starbucks."

Briscoe, who drank coffee at every opportunity, was about to accept when Malone cut him short. "No thanks. We'd just like to talk with Zelda."

Briscoe shot him with a look of disapproval.

"This is highly unusual," said the manger. "Couldn't you have contacted my employee at home rather than barge in here like this?"

Malone said, "We would have, sir. But we have no idea where Zelda lives. All we know is that one of your customers overheard her talking about an eagle that her husband shot. The customer called headquarters and reported it. All we have is her first name."

"Zelda is one of my top employees. I've known her for years. I'm surprised she'd be involved in something like this."

105

Briscoe said, "Maybe she didn't have a choice. Her husband shot the eagle. He's the one we're after, not her—"

There was a tap on the open door. They turned at once. A woman in her mid-thirties stood in the entranceway. Bone thin and auburn-haired with deep green eyes, her face grew incredulous when she saw the uniformed officers. "Is there something wrong?" she asked, thinking the worst. "Is Ben okay?"

The manager quickly answered: "Yes, yes, Zelda. He's fine. These are game wardens, not traffic cops. No one has been hurt. Please. Sit. They just want to talk to you for a moment."

Zelda walked into the room and sat on a folding chair, her hands folded tightly in her lap. Malone stepped around her and closed the office door. He pulled a chair next to her, sitting just outside her comfort zone. He motioned Briscoe to back away in an effort to put her at ease.

"I'm Officer Malone," he said in a relaxed, almost affable tone. He nodded over his shoulder at his partner. "Officer Briscoe and I are with the Pennsylvania Game Commission. We'd like to ask you a few questions."

"Ask *me* questions? Why? I'm not a hunter!"

"But your husband is, right?"

Zelda's eyes narrowed. "Yes," she said guardedly.

"We'd like to talk to you about the eagle."

"Eagle?"

"The eagle he shot."

Zelda's eyes widened into saucers. "Ben would never do something like that. My husband is a sportsman!"

Malone pushed on: "Would've been about a month ago...during deer season. Don't remember?"

"Remember what? I don't know what you're talking about!"

"Ma'am, we have a witness who overheard you telling a customer about it right in this store."

Zelda shook her head vigorously. "That's impossible! It never happened. Why would I tell somebody something that never happened? Your witness is either lying or has me confused with someone else."

Malone said, "Know anyone who has a vendetta against you or your husband? Someone who wants to get even?"

"Why, no. No one who would do anything like this! Look, I don't care what you think, but my husband is innocent. What's worse, my supervisor is sitting here right now, wondering if I'm some kind of pathological liar—"

"No, no, no, Zelda," the manager cut in. "I'm on your side. Really!"

Zelda looked at him. "I appreciate you saying that, but surely you must have some doubts. I know *I* would." She turned to Malone. "Look, you can search my house if you want. I only live ten minutes from here. You won't find anything but you're welcome to have a look."

Malone wasn't about to pass up the offer, and he didn't want to give Zelda time to call someone to get rid of any evidence. "Okay," he said. "We'd like to do it right now, though." He turned to her manager. "Would you allow Zelda to take some time off?"

The manager looked at Zelda. "Are you sure you want to do this?"

"Absolutely. I want to clear my husband's name and get on with my life. Can I go?"

"It's going to get busy soon," he cautioned. "Friday afternoons, you know."

Malone said, "We need a couple hours, sir. That's all."

He glanced at his wristwatch. "Fair enough. You've got two hours, Zelda. I'll have the other girls cover for you. Just make sure you're back on time."

**B**oyd Malone, Sam Briscoe and Claude Harper followed Zelda's jeep in Malone's cruiser as she proceeded through the only traffic light in town. The sky was bleak gray, a typical winter's day in northern Pennsylvania. Most of the snow had been cleared from the sidewalks and curbs, but the streets were covered in a heavy slush due to a recent, temporary thaw.

"This case is already a month old," Harper grumbled from the back seat. He was sitting with his arms folded tightly across his chest. "Odds are already against us, which is bad enough. But now we have a woman who willingly invites us into her home to look around. I don't think we're going to find a thing."

Malone glanced back at him through the rearview mirror, then focused on the road ahead "Let's see how it plays out, Claude. Her husband might've slipped a feather inside a book someplace. The way I heard it from dispatch, the informant sounded completely believable. We might find something after all."

Briscoe said, "Maybe a photograph or talons hidden in a bottom drawer. I'm betting he kept something—some kind of souvenir to remember it by."

Harper offered a half shrug of concession. "Possible, I guess. Hope you're right, because if we find anything like that, we're good to go. An eagle feather will fetch anywhere from five thousand to a hundred thousand in fines, even prison time depending on the circumstances. All we have to prove is possession to make a case; we don't have to show that he killed anything."

"Good," said Malone. "Because unless he admits to shooting it, which he most likely won't, we have a zero percent chance of proving he killed an eagle."

Malone swung a hard right and followed Zelda's jeep down a narrow, snow-covered road. She continued for another half mile until she pulled into a two-track leading to a small log house tucked back into the woods. She parked under a narrow carport and stood alongside her car while Malone pulled in behind her.

As they neared the front door, a man in his twenties stepped outside and stood on the porch with his hands on his hips. Although it was freezing outside, he wore only a T-shirt and jeans. "What's this all about, Zel?" he said, glaring at the wardens.

108

She stopped, the officers standing with her. Twenty feet separated them. "That's my brother, Zack," she muttered from the side of her mouth. "His bark is worse than his bite, but I want you to wait here for a moment." Zelda walked ahead, ascending three steps to a wood-framed landing, and faced him. "These men are conservation police officers," she said. "They want to search the house. They think I told someone at the store that Ben shot an eagle."

Zack's face fell into a frown, his voice a low hiss. "Why would they think something like that, Zelda? Could it be that you just plain talk too much?"

She stomped her foot, her whole body bristling. "But that's the thing, Zack! I never told anyone anything. Besides, the only thing Ben shot this winter was a deer. He would never kill an eagle! You know that! He always obeys the law."

Zack looked over at the wardens. "Three lawmen don't show up at your house unless they've got a reason. They must've heard something or they wouldn't be here. There's gotta be more to this then you're telling me."

"But there isn't, Zack. That's the crazy thing!"

"Then how did they get manage to get a search warrant?"

"I don't think they have one."

"Then tell them to leave! They got no right."

"This was *my* idea. I invited them here."

Zack stared at her in utter disbelief, his mouth forming a perfect O. "You did what?"

She'd had enough. "You need to back off, Zack. Do I have to remind you that you live here only because I choose to let you? Now step aside and let these gentlemen by. I have to get back to work, and I want this thing over with."


As far as Boyd Malone was concerned, the confrontation between Zelda and her brother only reinforced his conviction that he would find something. He followed her into the house along with Briscoe and Harper. Zack trailed behind without saying a word, his ego shattered by Zelda's stern reprimand.

They entered directly into the kitchen. Malone pulled a paper document from his coat pocket and handed it to Zelda.

"What's this?"

"It's a Consent to Search Form," said Malone, handing her a pen. "Need you to sign it. Protects both of us. It guarantees that you'll get a receipt for anything we find and assures us that you're okay with us coming into your house to search for evidence."

Zelda took a pair of glasses from her purse and slipped them on. She read over the form and scribbled her signature at the bottom.

"I'm fine with it," she said, handing the pen and paper back to Malone. "Ben's trophy room is in the back. That's what *he* calls it anyway. Believe me, if you're going to find anything, that's where it'll be."

The house was open to the living room and dining area with the floors finished in an attractive gunstock hardwood, the walls covered with a striking tongue and groove cedar paneling. Zelda escorted them through the living room to a short hallway that led to a bathroom and three bedrooms; the last bedroom had been converted to her husband's trophy room.

It was appropriately cluttered with all the trappings of a hardcore outdoorsman. The fierce head of a black bear hung dead center on an opposing wall, as if in guard over the abounding jumble. Another wall was decorated with archery equipment: longbows, compound bows, and crossbows suspended on wooden pegs. Various hunting rifles and shotguns ornamented a third wall, while another was reserved for mounted specimens collected over the years: dozens of deer racks were hung there, along with several full head mounts of trophy whitetails any hunter would have been proud to display. More archery equipment and firearms were stacked in corners along with crates of ammunition, reloading equipment, camouflage clothing, and related paraphernalia.

The officers began their search, looking for any possible link to the eagle. A feather tucked neatly under some folded garment would be all they'd need to make a case. They poked and probed through hunting coats and canvass pants scrutinizing every inch of cloth. Ammo boxes were opened and drawers sorted through. Nothing would be overlooked.

But as the men busily searched, their backs turned to Zelda, she let out a sudden scream that ran through them like a buzz saw.

Malone whipped his head in Zelda's direction, eyes following the aim of her finger.

"Look! Look!" she cried. "I remember now! He did shoot an eagle!"

She was pointing at an old canvass golf bag leaning in a corner.

*Could the eagle be hidden inside?* thought Malone.

"It was the golf tournament!" she announced triumphantly. "He shot an eagle at the golf tournament last fall! That's what I was talking about at the store!"

Malone looked at Brisco, his face a map of surprise and bewilderment. *"What the...?"*

Briscoe rolled his eyes in disbelief. "That's golf lingo for two under par," he said dryly.

The revelation hit Malone like a freight train. He looked at the federal agent. "I can't believe this," he said, shaking his head in despair. "Never in my wildest dreams would I have thought—"

"Wait till the headquarters hears about this," Harper cut in. "I'm gonna pay big-time."

Briscoe and Harper glanced over at Zelda and saw an expression of relief on her face. And there was something else: a twinkle in her eye that told them she found the whole thing somewhat amusing now that it was over. This became an instant green light for Briscoe, and he turned to Harper with a mischievous smirk.

"Any openings in the Fish and Wildlife Service for crack investigators?" he said. "Malone might be looking for a place to hang his hat for a while."

Harper paused for a moment before nodding tentatively. "I hear there's an opening near Nome, Alaska. It's remote, the winters are paralyzing, and the landscape is bleak—completely barren as a matter of fact. But there's a bright side."

"What's that?" asked Briscoe.

"It's too cold for bald eagles and the closest golf course is five hundred miles away."

Zelda giggled softly, then quickly covered her mouth with her hand, trying not to add to Malone's embarrassment. But his forlorn expression was more than she could bear, and she soon burst out in bright laughter.

And the three wardens, relieved by her good humor, couldn't help but laugh along with her.

# Anatomy of a Shooting

GOLDEN FINGERS OF SUNLIGHT STREAKED the cold and gray November skyline as Serge Laflame made his way through the awakening forest. Dawn was breaking, and his heart began to pound with excitement. He had been waiting for the season opener, it seemed, for an eternity, and had spent a sleepless night in anticipation of this day. Although he was in his forties and a hunter most of his life, turkey season still held a special place in his heart. No other game bird or animal excited him more.

There were reports of big gobblers in Possum Hollow. Trophy gobblers with beards that touched the ground and body weights approaching thirty pounds. Up until now, Serge could only dream of taking such a fine bird. But today would be different. Not a single vehicle was parked anywhere near this place. And to Serge Laflame, that meant he had the hollow all to himself. This would be his special day. He could feel it in his bones. A day he would remember for years to come.

He froze suddenly. Scarcely breathing, he stood statue-like, fingers curling tightly against the fore-end of his shotgun, eyes searching the trees. A lifetime in the woods told him there were turkeys here. He listened but heard nothing. Looked but saw nothing. Still, something made him pause. Some unidentified sixth sense that broke his stride as if an electric switch had been thrown. The woods had become eerily silent, and he could almost hear the blood coursing through his veins as he scanned the branches above with a slow and deliberate scrutiny.

They exploded from a tall oak behind him. A dozen black shadows in the early dawn. Wings beating the air like blankets flapping in a storm. Serge turned and quickly shouldered his gun, trigger finger set as he took aim. But these were medium birds, not the longbeards he'd come for, and he slowly brought his shotgun to rest.

Then another turkey burst from a distant pine. It rocketed through the dim forest, skirting trees with the faultless precision of a heat-seeking missile. Too late for a clear shot, Serge watched the trophy gobbler break deep into the woods and set its broad wings before disappearing into the hollow. He stood on his toes, eyes straining, hoping to see where the bird would land. Then he moved on in eager pursuit.

Tobias Rono was a big man: six five and a solid two hundred and fifty pounds, his broad back resting against a great white oak. Dressed in full camouflage, orange safety hat on the ground next to him, he had been sitting patiently in Possum Hollow for more than an hour. Like Serge Laflame, he too had been counting the days until the season finally opened. Turkey hunting was his passion. He'd been up since four in the morning, and with a hurried breakfast under his belt, he was out the door in less than an hour. The hollow was a short drive from his home, and he had managed to obtain permission to hunt a section of posted property that a friend recently purchased. After parking his jeep, Tobias walked through the woods in the dark for a good half mile before settling down. As the only hunter allowed on the property, he would have the place all to himself.

And when Tobias heard the turkey touch down, he started to work his magic on the trusty box call he'd used so successfully over the past twenty years. This was the moment he'd been waiting for. With a series of low clucks, he would lure the bird to him like the mythical Pied Piper of Hamelin. Ah, yes. It was going to be a very good day, he thought. A very good day indeed.

Serge Laflame continued through the trees lined with No Trespassing posters as he moved toward his quarry. These were new. He'd been here earlier in the year scouting for fresh sign. The entire hollow had been open then. Now some newcomer moved in and posted his property. Not fair. Not fair at all. Serge had been hunting here for years, and he wasn't about to let a few posters get in his way. After all, who would know? He hadn't seen a soul all morning. Besides, sweet success was so close now. He could hear the turkey up ahead, making a low clucking sound. Surely that was the bird he'd flushed.

He had walked past the posters with barely another glance at them. And with those first few steps, the fact that he'd turned from hunter to poacher never entered his mind. Instead, he envisioned the stares of wide-eyed admiration he'd receive from friends and family when he returned home with his trophy. Slowly and methodically, he would continue his pursuit, moving with cautious, almost fluid precision, until the bird of his dreams was finally in view.

He was close now. Very close. The soft purrs and clucks had come from behind a white oak just twenty yards ahead. He froze, eyes boring into the forest for a glimpse of his prize as he brought his twelve-gauge to his shoulder. Soon it would show itself, and it would be a clear shot from where he stood. This time he'd make sure it didn't get away. With his finger on the trigger, he would be quick to squeeze off a shot at first sight of the bird.

Tobias Rono, all but invisible in his camouflage clothing, saw something from the corner of his eye. A fleeting movement, a mere shadow in the forest. What was it? Slowly, he turned his head to see.

And as he did, the mottled pattern of his facemask transformed into the feathers of a turkey.

Tobias Rono saw him suddenly, a shotgun at his shoulder. Impossible! It was pointed right at him! He quickly turned his face, instinctively closing his eyes, bracing himself for the impact that would come.

And that second movement—although it spared him from blindness—was all it took for Serge Laflame to squeeze the trigger. He fired immediately at the fleeing turkey. His twelve-gauge, loaded with three-inch magnum rounds, discharging its terrible charge into Tobias Rono's face, neck, and shoulder. The blast lifted him off the ground, the copper-plated pellets taking many of his teeth and narrowly missing his eyes.

Tobias Rono lay on the forest floor writhing in pain. His head felt like it had been run over by a truck. Blood streamed from the wounds in his face and neck as he struggled to get to his feet. He felt something wet and warm inside his coat, saturating his right arm. Blood. Too much blood. He tried to pull himself up, to run for help, but when he got to his knees the forest started spinning like a carousel. Dazed and in a state of shock, Tobias Rono fell to the ground in the open woods and cried out for help.

Serge Laflame never heard a human voice; instead, he heard only the high-pitched yelps of a distressed turkey. He quickly pumped another magnum round into his shotgun and charged recklessly toward his quarry. But within seconds, he stopped dead in his tracks. He saw the body of a man where a turkey had been moments ago. And the sick realization that he had just shot a human being came crashing down upon him like a gigantic wave.

As a state game warden, an important part of my job was the investigation of hunting related shooting incidents, commonly referred to as hunting accidents. Although an unpleasant task, due to the human tragedy surrounding most cases, it was also fascinating work. Investigating a shooting incident can be intriguing: What caused it? How could it have been prevented? Was it an accident occurring by mere chance, or did it develop from sheer negligence?

I learned over the years that most hunting-related shooting incidents are caused through negligence, often fueled by the offender's intense desire to harvest a game animal at almost any cost. And, unlike many might suspect, it's not the inexperienced hunter who is responsible for most of these incidents. In many cases, the offender is someone who has hunted for many years, and he is generally hunting with a shotgun, in broad daylight, for turkey or small game when it happens.

Unfortunately, there will always be some who measure the success of a hunt by what they can kill. Return without game and the day is a loss they reason. The wise sportsman chooses his hunting companions carefully, avoiding those who consider a hunting trip unsuccessful unless they bag something. Such individuals are too quick to pull the trigger, and as we all know, there is no eraser on the end of a gun. One tiny movement of your index finger can change your life—as well as your victim's—forever.

When my radio blurted the message about a shooting, I was forty miles away, and by the time I got there, the victim had already been transported to a hospital. Arrangements for the Medevac flight had been made by state troopers who arrived long before I did. They escorted me to a PSP cruiser where Laflame was being held for questioning and I took him into my custody. Because the victim was unconscious and critically injured, I couldn't interview him for at least another day.

I was truly shocked when Serge Laflame admitted chambering another shell and running toward Tobias Rono after shooting him in mistake for a turkey. I had investigated dozens of shooting incidents up until that time, many involving humans shot in mistake for game, but this was the first time I'd come across an offender who was ready to fire a second round without realizing that he'd shot a human.

Laflame was knowingly trespassing on private posted property when he came upon Tobias Rono. And although hunting accidents can and do happen to honest, law-abiding hunters, I've found they often coincide with some kind of illegal hunting activity.

When poachers are pursuing game, their goal is to kill quickly and disappear quickly in order to avoid detection. They are often careless in their haste, which increases the possibility that a stray bullet might hit someone, as most poachers are not thinking about who or what might be in their line of fire. Their reckless disregard for safety also increases the likelihood that they'll mistake a human for game. Poachers are not fond of blaze orange clothing, either. Although often required by state game laws, so hunters will be more visible, poachers don't want to be seen. As a result, they are more likely to be victims of hunting accidents as well.

But the question remains, poacher or honest hunter, how can someone shoot a human being in mistake for a turkey? People don't have wings! And for that matter, how can someone shoot a human in mistake for a deer, a bear, or any other animal? For we don't have antlers, hairy coats, or four legs, either.

I once investigated an incident where a hunter shot someone in mistake for a squirrel. Sounds impossible, right? In this case, a bow hunter out for deer was dressed in full camouflage while standing on a tree branch twenty feet in the air. A squirrel hunter happened by and never saw the archer because his camouflage clothing blended so well with the tree's canopy. The squirrel hunter looked up, mistook the bottom of archer's boot for a gray squirrel, and shot him through the foot with a twenty-two caliber rifle. Still, a boot does not a squirrel make. One is bare rubber, the other covered with fur—and has a tail! So, again, how does this happen?

It is my belief that people who shoot someone in mistake for game don't see a true picture of their surroundings. Instead, they perceive mental images that they *want* to see, due to an overwhelming desire for "success." These perceptions are reinforced by a logical chain of events—actual happenings—that bolster their convictions right up to the moment that they pull the trigger. In other words, real events integrate with the imagined, producing mental images that are projected in the mind, much like a video on a television screen.

Many psychologists agree that as we go through life we create a mental blueprint of how things should work for us. That is, we sense the real world around us, but our sensations are based on individual and unique perceptions of our surroundings. Simply stated, we recognize and interpret happenings based on what we believe rather than what is actual. Interestingly, psychologists emphasize that human perception is complicated by technologies such as camouflage, citing the example of Peacock butterflies, whose wings have eye markings that birds react to as though they belonged to the eyes of a predator. In humans, this reaction is called imagination, which is our inborn ability to create partial or complete imaginary worlds within the mind from sense perceptions of the real world. Psychologists say that these realms or images are seen with what's commonly referred to as the mind's eye.

I am convinced that if every hunter practiced two basic rules of safe hunting, far fewer humans would be shot in mistake for game. The first is to positively identify your target. As detailed above, under the right circumstances, your mind can play tricks on you. And while the psychology of human perceptions can be difficult to grasp, we are all familiar with common optical illusions such as paper drawings with figures that seem to move about or appear three-dimensional when you know, in fact, that they are not. Have you ever mistakenly identified a tree stump or a rock for some kind of bird or animal? I have. It's a common optical illusion that many of us have experienced at least once in our lives.

Although most hunters are careful and take plenty of time to absorb what they see, some don't. They simply react. As a result, humans are shot in mistake for game birds and animals each year, bringing tragic results to both the victim and offender.

Therefore, it is imperative not only to positively identify your target as a legal game animal but also to be seen. To accomplish this, you must take measures to stand out from your natural surroundings. Fluorescent orange has proven to be extremely effective in protecting hunters from being shot, especially in mistake for game. For that reason, whenever the law allows you to remove your orange clothing after reaching your calling position, you should always display a fluorescent orange alert band nearby, especially if you plan to call or use decoys. It may save your life.

In fact, in every incident I ever investigated involving a hunter shot in mistake for game, he was posted in a wooded area, dressed in full camouflage, and failed to display any fluorescent orange material.

An additional contributing factor to these shooting incidents was the victim's movement, however slight, as in the Serge Laflame case. Consequently, if you sense another hunter coming your way, you must remain motionless. Always suspect he may be stalking you. Do not wave (especially your orange hat, which can be mistaken for the wattles on a turkey) at anyone as a signal. Instead, shout, "STOP!" Make sure that the individual is aware of your presence and that he is safely relocated before resuming your hunt.

Statistics show that the number of incidents where hunters are shot in mistake for game ranks second only to those shot in the line of fire, with negligence upon the offender being the primary factor. Line-of-fire shootings are more difficult to protect yourself from because, in some instances, heavy brush or hilly terrain can make it impossible for others to see you even if you're wearing fluorescent orange clothing from head to toe. Hence, the wise hunter is always conscious of what lies beyond his target, and refrains from shooting at game on horizons. Unfortunately, I've investigated many line-of-fire incidents where hunters have been shot at close range while in plain view of the offender. In these cases, even a simple orange hat could have prevented the incident.

I'll never forget the time a hunter shot his companion while they were on opposite sides of a small pond. The men were hunting together when they spotted several ducks on the water up ahead. Deciding to split up, they kept low and approached the birds. Both men stood directly across from each other with shotguns at the ready when the ducks suddenly lifted off. Nothing but forty yards of clean air and a few mallards separated them when a shot was fired. The victim, on the opposite side of the pond, was struck from his neck to his knees with seventy lead pellets.

He was able to talk to me when I arrived at the hospital later that afternoon. Although in considerable pain, he managed a faint smile as I walked into the room. He was lying in bed, covered in a flimsy johnnie exposing arms peppered with raw, nasty looking puncture wounds.

"Not exactly a day at the beach," I said.

He barked a hoarse chuckle. "Hurts like hell, too!"

More serious now, I said, "Are you okay? Can we talk?"

"Sure."

"This was an accident, right?" I said. "I mean, you were only forty yards apart, in plain view of each other. Sun was up; lighting conditions were excellent. He had to see you."

"But he didn't...somehow. We've been hunting together for years. We're good friends, officer. He's all shook up over this. Taking it worse than I am. No, it was an accident all right—he wasn't trying to kill me if that's what you're getting at."

"Had to ask. Part of the job."

"I know. I'd be thinking the same thing if I were you."

I asked a few more questions and then walked out to the lobby where his partner was seated in a stuffed chair, elbows on knees, holding his head as if suffering from a migraine. I sat next to him and introduced myself.

"I can't believe it," he said, shaking his head with regret. "He's my best friend and I put him in the hospital. I never thought I'd make a mistake like this."

"How did it happen?"

He shrugged his shoulders and wiped a tear from his cheek. "I swear I never even saw him. Should have. But I didn't. When the ducks took flight, I did a quick point-and-shoot. Next thing I know, Jim is lying on the ground screaming in pain. It's like a nightmare. Only it's not, it's real. All I can say is thank God he's not blind...or even dead.

One inch, warden. If I'd have raised the barrel another inch I would have hit him square in the face."

Inexcusable as they may be, line-of-fire incidents like this occur because the offender sees his target and nothing else. Science has shown that instances of intense, psychological emotion can trigger the onset of tunnel vision, causing someone to sharply narrow his field of vision (or focus) to the point that he is visualizing his surroundings as if looking through the scope on a hunting rifle.

This may explain how an overzealous hunter might shoot someone who is plainly visible and in his direct line of fire, if the hunter's sole objective is to bag a piece of game before it gets away.

Another example, similar to the duck hunting episode, was an incident I investigated involving two brothers who were hunting on private property without permission. It was archery season; the men were in a wooded area mixed with a heavy undergrowth of shrubs and saplings known to be overrun with deer. They were in a hurry to make a kill and get out before being discovered. I'll call them Ben and Jerry from this point on.

The men decided to split up, one going north while the other worked his way south. Both were dressed in camouflage clothing and had made no specific plans as to where they'd set up. A short time after parting, Jerry came to a waterway too deep to cross and began to work his way back toward Ben. Unfortunately, he never bothered to signal his brother to let him know.

When Ben saw two deer coming his way, he raised his bow and took aim, following their course through an opening to his left. The bigger deer, a trophy buck, was in the lead. Ben zeroed in and quickly released his draw before the buck could disappear into the thick understory. But in his haste, his arrow missed, sailing just over the deer's shoulder.

Although a mere fifty yards separated them, Ben never saw his brother standing in plain view opposite the deer, and his razor-edged broadhead plunged into Jerry's left bicep, severing his brachial artery and penetrating into bone.

Horrified by his brutal injury and in a state of shock, Jerry screamed out. He grabbed the wooden shaft and ripped the steel broadhead from his arm, creating even more tissue damage and loss of blood as the wedge-shaped arrowhead backed out of his flesh.

Hearing his brother's screams, Ben threw his bow to the ground and ran to him, nearly blacking out when he saw his gaping wound. Jerry was kneeling on the ground, head low, white as a ghost. He looked like he was about to faint. A jagged chunk of muscle tissue flapped back over his bicep from where the arrow had been yanked out. Blood spurted in great crimson arcs. Ben tore off his shirt, then his undershirt. He wrapped the garment tightly around his brother's arm and tied it there. He forced him to his feet and held him close.

"Jerry! Snap out of it, man. Work with me!" he cried. "We gotta get out of here—get you to a doctor."

The brothers stumbled awkwardly through the woods, side by side, Ben's strong arm reaching across Jerry's back and tucking under his armpit to support him. He glanced at his white undershirt, now turned red with his brother's blood. Then he prayed, as all men do when overwhelmed by fear.

It was with tremendous good fortune that they were hunting—albeit unlawfully—on land that belonged to a large hospital. They were only two hundred yards from the parking lot. And in the distance, Ben could make out a sign through the trees that said EMERGENCY ENTRANCE.

But Jerry was fading fast, and a distance of but two football fields became a torturous ordeal, as Ben was forced to support more and more of his brother's weight. Jerry had become unresponsive, eyes flat and vacant as he staggered drunkenly under Ben's strong arm. But Ben was tiring fast. He stopped for a moment to collect his breath, heart pounding from exertion, feeling guilty not to be pushing on. But it was either that or risk losing consciousness from his labor. Too many cigarettes over the years had taken their toll. He carefully lowered his brother to the ground and put him in a seated position with his back against a tree for support. He sat with him, his chest heaving to feed his aching lungs.

A horn honked in the parking lot ahead. He could hear the whoosh of vehicles as they traveled the highway bordering the hospital. So many people. So close. Yet unable to help. How could they? No one knew they were here. Utterly exhausted, he looked at his semi-conscious brother. Blood dripped from his bandaged arm, peppering the leaf cover with bright red spatters.

Again he prayed. Bowing his head, he closed his eyes and asked God for the strength to carry his beloved brother to safety. Promising to be a better man if only—

"Ben?"

He paused.

"Help me."

He looked.

Jerry's hand was extended toward him, eyes somehow clear and alert. "I don't have much time."

Ben stood and took his brother's arm, pulling him to his feet. He willed his legs to walk as they stumbled over fallen branches and jagged rocks along the way, arms locked around each other for support. The final minutes it took to clear the woods seemed an eternity. And when their feet finally touched macadam, they had only reached the remote parking area. The hospital loomed in the distance, and Jerry's body, soaked in blood, had become so limp that Ben could barely hold him. And for a moment, he almost gave up hope.

There was the beep of a horn!

Ben whipped his head around. A car almost touching him. And a woman suddenly standing there.

"I've got 'em," she said.

Ben's mind was spinning. He couldn't remember her taking his brother from his grip, but suddenly she was holding him under both arms, his body sagging under its own weight. He was unconscious, his head hung to one side, complexion deathly white.

"Help me get him in my car. Hurry!" the woman said.

Ben grabbed Jerry's legs and together they laid him on the back seat. Ben slid inside with him as the woman got behind the wheel.

She raced to the hospital's emergency entrance. Together they carried Jerry's lifeless body through a glass sliding door. Nurses swarmed around them from every direction. A doctor appeared from out of nowhere.

"Get this man into surgery, stat!" he barked.

Orderlies appeared and put Jerry's body on a gurney. They wheeled him down a narrow corridor, twin wooden doors bursting open as they disappeared into the operating room. Ben stood woodenly and watched, his eyes staring down the vacant hallway long after they were gone.

The following day, I interviewed the surgeon who worked on Jerry for five long hours taking a vein from his leg to graft it to his brachial artery, a procedure commonly used with open bypass surgery patients suffering from heart disease. The surgeon told me that Jerry had lost so much blood from his wound it was a miracle he survived.

"He had a lot of luck going for him," he said. "If that woman hadn't come by to drive them to the emergency room, he would've been dead before we got him into surgery. It was that close."

"Interesting," I said, "because I spoke with his brother earlier today, and he has no idea who she was. He said she left before he could thank her. Said he turned around to shake her hand and she was gone."

The surgeon smiled indifferently. "Happens," he said. "More than you might think. Good Samaritans who simply want to be left out of the spotlight. The man definitely had a guardian angel looking out for him, though."

"Yes, I guess he did."

I never did find out who the woman was that helped save Jerry's life. But then, had a few common safety tips been followed, there would have been no trip to the hospital in the first place.

Just like the duck hunters before them, Ben and Jerry had put themselves into each other's zone of fire. This is never good. And in both instances, the shooters focused exclusively on their targets without giving any consideration to what might lie beyond. This is inexcusable no matter how you look at it. I'm also certain that had the victims been wearing even a minimal amount of fluorescent orange clothing they wouldn't have been shot.

In the three decades that I spent investigating hunting accidents, I learned that seasoned hunters, sometimes with forty or more years' experience, are more likely to be involved in hunting related shooting incidents than novice hunters. And while I've heard every imaginable explanation and excuse from both victims and offenders over the years, the one thing I never heard anyone say is, "I knew this would happen to me one day."

Think about that.

Fact is, it can happen to just about anyone, especially if they believe it can't.

# Deceit, Lies, and Alibis

**W**ITH PRACTICE, a law enforcement officer can become very effective at ferreting out the truth simply by observing an individual's facial expressions and body gestures. The ability to read a suspect while conducting an interview can be a tremendous asset to an investigator, as a person's subconscious behavior, or body language as it's often called, can help bring a successful conclusion to a case.

I remember the opening day of doe season, back in 1976, when I received a phone call about a man attempting to kill a second deer. In those days, a hunter could only take one deer, buck or doe, per season. Pennsylvania had over a million licensed hunters back then, and although we were called game wardens by most, our official title was GAME PROTECTOR, as inscribed on our badges and arm patches. Cell phones and personal computers were virtually unheard of, and we typed our reports on manual typewriters. If you didn't know how to spell, it showed, as there was no such thing as spellcheck; hence, I confess to spending considerable time perusing the two-inch thick dictionary that lay beside my Smith Corona typewriter. Our home phone numbers were published each year in the Pennsylvania Hunting and Trapping Digest, which was issued along with every hunting license sold. And because I was assigned to a territory encompassing both Philadelphia and Montgomery Counties at the time, with a population approaching three million, I received thousands of calls and complaints each year.

And with those calls came a certain number of cranks who found it entertaining to sick the game warden on people they didn't like by falsely claiming they were poaching deer. Happened every year. So when the anonymous call came one Saturday alleging that a man had killed a buck and was back on the same property hunting for doe, I took it with a grain of salt.

"What's his name?" I asked the complainant.

"His name is Tommy Dyce. I work with the guy. See him most every day."

"Where do you work?"

"I don't want to say, but I'll tell you this: He's been bragging about the buck he killed last week and now he's after a doe. I'm a welder up the line from him. He don't know I can hear him, but he's a loud mouth, and I can hear him real good. That's how I know where he hunts. It's a farm in Upper Dublin Township. Went by there just a few minutes ago. I'm telling you he's looking to kill another deer right now. His truck is parked next to the barn, a red Dodge Power Wagon. Can't miss it."

Although my district was primarily urban, and consequently designated a "buckshot only" zone by the Game Commission, there were many large tracts of woods and reverting farms overrun with deer. And that, coupled with the considerable human population, produced more hunting pressure than you might imagine. The large deer herd also tempted more than a few unscrupulous hunters to try for a second buck or doe. After all, they reasoned, what difference would it make—there were so many deer, who would miss them? Problem is, if everyone thought that way our deer herd would have been decimated long ago.

The key to successful hunting in Montgomery County was—and still is—to gain access to some of the large private holdings in the area rather than join the legions of hunters beating the brush for deer inhabiting the few state properties that permitted hunting. Although working farms were few and far between, many sprawling estates dotted the area, and they were often overrun with deer. Here you could enjoy the luxury of relative obscurity from the roaming eye of the law. According to my informant, Mr. Dyce had managed to find his way into one of these places and was taking full advantage of his good fortune.

I donned my uniform, jumped into my forest green patrol car, and started down the highway toward Upper Dublin Township, wondering all the while if this would end up being a wild goose chase. Traffic was heavy, and it took a good half hour to reach the farm.

The property, a hundred acres or so, consisted primarily of heavy scrub brush with a good-sized patch of woods at the rear. There was an old house and barn just off the road, and as I drove down the winding dirt driveway, I spotted a red Dodge Power Wagon parked next to the barn, telling me that my suspect was still in the area. I parked by the truck and climbed out of my vehicle under a blue December sky. Unusual for the time of year, there was no snow on the ground. In fact, not a single flake had fallen so far that winter. The air was calm but cold, and I could see someone a hundred yards away in an open meadow, the sun reflecting brightly upon his blaze orange coat and hat. He was cradling a shotgun, and I started walking toward him.

He saw me coming and froze in his tracks. As a rule, most hunters are a bit hesitant when a game warden approaches, but there was something about this man's rigid posture that said he was more annoyed than alarmed. He stood stiff as a post, his shotgun gripped in a forty-five degree angle across his chest like a shield. At twenty-five yards I paused and turned my upper body to the right, pretending to glance over my shoulder so he wouldn't notice as I flipped open the snap on my holstered three-fifty-seven magnum revolver.

Approaching armed hunters is a routine, daily occurrence for game wardens during hunting season. But with it comes a greater danger of being killed in action than any other police job in the country. Although odds are against it, as most hunters are honest, law-abiding citizens, game wardens are potential sitting ducks for anyone who wants to shoot at us as we approach on foot. Although in this particular case I had prepared myself for a quick draw if necessary, in reality my chances of survival against a shotgun with no barriers between me and my assailant were minimal at best.

Earlier in my career, I learned of a tragic incident where a father took his ten-year-old son for a walk in the woods and killed him with his shotgun. Then, turning the gun on himself, he took his own life. It happened in a wooded area not far from my home, and I often wondered what would have happened had I approached them that day, thinking they were out for a hunt. Only two conclusions came to mind: either I would have been shot and killed or I would have prevented the tragedy from happening. That was almost forty years ago, but the thought still haunts me to this day, and it kept me ever cautious throughout my career whenever I approached an armed hunter.

Moving forward, I called out, "State game warden! Keep your barrel in the air and unload your firearm!"

Muzzle pointed skyward, I watched him ratchet his pump shotgun. Three high brass shells ejected from the magazine to lay at his feet as he continued working the action to show there were no additional rounds. He squatted and picked up his shells, dropping them into his coat pocket. Then he stood and stared at me with a wrinkled brow as I approached. "Don't you have anything better to do than traipse out here and ruin my hunt?" he said.

His belligerent attitude didn't surprise me. Some poachers are hostile, others meek, when confronted by a game warden. Dyce, apparently, was the aggressive type.

"Turn around," I said. "I want to see your hunting license."

He shook his head with contempt, then pivoted, turning his back so I could pull his license from its plastic holder. As soon as I removed it, he spun around. "You should be out catching poachers not harassing honest hunters!" he snarled.

His eyes were crystal blue, which made his stony glare all the more piercing. In his late twenties, he was clean shaven except for a thin wisp of a mustache, his tall and narrow frame suggesting a weight of perhaps a hundred-and-seventy pounds or so. I flipped open the cardboard license and looked at the name inside. "Thomas Dyce," I said, glancing up at him.

He frowned impatiently. "That's right."

I noticed that the perforated deer tag, although still attached to his license, had been filled out in pencil and partially erased: the date, time of kill, and antler information rubbed out. It had been hastily done, and I could read everything that had been previously entered.

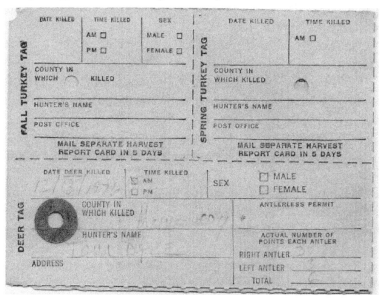

Dyce had killed a buck one week earlier, three points on each antler according to the information that had been on the tag. Erasing a tag was a common practice among poachers in those days. However, most did a much better job than Dyce did by being mindful to pencil-in the information lightly enough to be rubbed completely clean later. And the fact that the tag was still attached to the license told me it was a premeditated act. By law, tags are supposed to be detached from the license—which is why they're conveniently perforated—and then affixed to the ear of a deer immediately after removing the entrails. A hunting license with a missing tag is highly noticeable, making it blatantly obvious that a deer has been taken. Dyce's tag remained attached to his license so he could affix the whole thing to the deer's ear with the tag filled out. That way, if a game warden stopped him on a routine field check, he would play dumb and beg to be excused for not detaching the tag, claiming it was an innocent mistake. Once home, he erased whatever he wanted so the tag could be reused. I don't know where the convoluted idea came from, but I'd run across my share of hunters doing this sort of thing. I never gave any of them a break.

"It looks like you already killed a deer," I said. "You shouldn't be hunting today."

His eyes narrowed. "What are you talking about? I didn't kill any deer."

"Oh, I think you did. A six-point buck, in fact. You didn't do a very good job of erasing your tag. I can still see where you wrote three points for each antler."

He extended a hand. "Let me see that."

I played along and gave back his license, curious about what he'd say next.

He glanced at it, then shoved his license back at me as if it were toxic. "That wasn't me!" he said with mocked indignation. "One of my kids did that. They were playing with it the other day."

Not too original, I thought. For I'd heard the same flimsy excuse almost every time I came upon a hunter with an altered tag.

"I don't think so," I said. "I'm not here by accident. I have reliable information that you already killed a buck."

Dyce looked at me as if I'd just accused him of being a pedophile. "That's ridiculous!"

Pocketing his license I said, "You're done hunting today."

The veins in his neck bulged, his face flushed with anger. "I know a little about the law," he barked. "If you think I killed a deer you'll just have to prove it."

I was certain that if I'd told him a fellow employee overheard him bragging at work about it, he would have taken a different attitude. But my informant wanted to remain anonymous, and I had to honor his request even if it meant Dyce might walk free.

Talking any further seemed useless. I told him to hand over his shotgun and the three shells he'd put in his pocket.

He balked at my request. "What for?"

"Evidence for the charges I'll be filing."

"What charges?"

"Attempting to kill a second deer and altering a hunting license, for starters."

"Look, you got no right to take my—"

"I got every right!" I said, cutting him off. "And unless you want me to add interfering with an officer to your charges and place you under arrest, you better start cooperating!"

I'd had enough for one day, and Dyce could tell by my tone that I was dead serious. With a scowl of submission, he handed me his shotgun and then dug into his pocket for the shells. I took them from him and walked back to my patrol car, leaving him in the field with no license and no gun.

Even without a confession, I still had a few options remaining to build a case against him. Deputy Tom Scarpello was patrolling nearby. I grabbed my mike and radioed out to him, asking that he check on the deer processors in the area to see if Dyce brought in a buck last week. It was a longshot, as many hunters cut up their own deer, but if someone had a record of his kill, it would help bring my case to a successful conclusion.

While Scarpello was canvassing area deer processors, I walked over to the landowner's house, hoping someone could answer a few questions about Mr. Dyce. I knocked and soon an elderly woman came to the door. Arthritic and bent at the hips, she stood in the doorway and eyed my uniform uneasily.

"Morning, ma'am," I said. "I'm Officer Wasserman with the state game commission. Did you give a man named Tom Dyce permission to hunt here?"

"Why, yes," she said cautiously. Her hands were clasped tightly, a crooked thumb shifting nervously over pallid knuckles. "What's this all about?"

"Do you recall whether or not he killed a deer?"

She frowned in thought for a moment, then looked over my shoulder and stared into the distant horizon.

It was as if she'd fallen into a trance, and I didn't know if she would respond to my question, when an elderly man stepped into the doorway beside her.

"Excuse me for interrupting, officer," he said. "I couldn't help overhearing your question. The gentleman you speak of most certainly killed a deer here; he thanked us profusely for allowing him to hunt on our land." Turning his head to toward the woman, he said, "Don't you remember, Helen? Why, he even came back later with some venison steaks for us. They were delicious. Surely you remember that."

The old woman rolled her eyes in resignation. "Oh! Why, yes. Yes, of course. I remember now." She scowled at him. "Thank you for reminding me, Peter!"

Peter's head retracted into his shoulders. Then he turned from the doorway and disappeared into the darkened house.

The woman smiled icily. "Now, if you'll excuse me, officer, it's time for my medication."

An engine started behind me. I did an about-face and watched Tom Dyce back his truck away from the barn and wheel toward the state highway. When I turned around, I came face-to-face with a closed door. Meeting adjourned.

Although I didn't think the elderly couple would show up for a court case, even if subpoenaed by a judge, I intended to use the information they'd given me as a lever against Dyce the next time I met with him.

As I got back into my patrol car and started toward the highway, my radio started to crackle. It was Deputy Scarpello calling to say he found a processor who butchered a deer for Tom Dyce. Scarpello relayed the address to me, and I started in that direction to interview the owner.

It was a short three-mile drive with no traffic, unusual for Montgomery County. The butcher shop was located in a detached two-car garage that had been converted into a temporary deer processing business for the hunting season. Just off the highway, it sat next to a small single-story brick house. A hand-made sign hung over closed garage doors: HARRY'S DEER PROCESSING.

When I pulled into the driveway, a man in his fifties stepped out of a side entrance doorway to greet me. He had a large brushy mustache flecked with gray, his hair trimmed soldier short. A bloodstained polyester bib-apron covered his brown flannel shirt and blue jeans.

"I'm Harry Smothers," he said. "Your deputy said you'd be here. Come on in."

I followed him inside the garage. A clear vinyl curtain divided the place in two. I could see three gutted deer hanging by their hocks from steel grapples on the other side.

"They're all tagged and legal," said Harry. "Your deputy inspected them when he was here." He walked past a stainless steel bandsaw, its thin blade speckled with tiny particles of meat, and grabbed a loose-leaf binder from a Formica cutting table. "My record book," he said. He opened it on the table and turned to the third page. "Yep. Here he is. Tom Dyce brought in a six-point buck." He picked the binder off the table and handed it to me. "See for yourself."

I looked at the entry and handed it back.

Harry said, "He stops in every year with a buck for me to cut up. Steaks, deer-burger and jerky. That's the way he likes it. Must be in trouble, huh? Else you wouldn't be here."

I nodded. "Did he ever ask you to do a second deer?"

"No. He knows better than that. Anybody brings an illegal deer into my place, I throw 'em out. But there's lots of processors besides me around. A smart guy would go see one of them if he wanted a second deer cut up."

There was no doubt about Dyce's guilt at this point, but without a confession, I would have to subpoena Harry Smothers and the elderly couple at the house to testify against him in court. I would only do that as a last resort, but didn't think it would be necessary. I was sure Tom Dyce would talk once I confronted him with the information I'd acquired.

Thinking Dyce might have gone straight home after leaving the farm, I drove by his house and spotted his truck

135

parked in the street out front. As I pulled up behind it, Tom Dyce walked out the front door and met me at the curb.

"Been expecting you," he said. "When I saw you talking to Helen and Peter I knew it was over."

"Nice people," I said. "Informative too."

He winced. "Helen's my aunt. Wasn't worried about her, she's a cool customer. Peter, on the other hand, is an entirely different matter. My uncle and I don't get along. Figured he'd ruin it for me."

"He's not the only one," I said. "I just left Harry Smothers' place. Saw his record book."

Dyce dropped his gaze and blew a long sigh. "Yep. He butchered a buck for me, all right. I didn't find the carcass until the next day. Foxes got to it first. Not a whole lot left for me, so that's why I tried for another deer today."

I said, "It's a two hundred dollar violation. You can pay on a field acknowledgement of guilt or take a hearing. Your choice. But if we go to court, I'll subpoena your aunt and uncle. Harry Smothers too."

"I don't want that," he said. "Helen will never let me hunt on her property again. I'll just pay the fine. You got me."

"I'll be settling cases at the state police barracks in Limerick next Saturday at one o'clock," I said. "Ask for me and a deputy will escort you back to my room."

Confident Dyce would show up to pay his fine, I got back into my vehicle and resumed my patrol, stopping by Harry Smothers' shop along the way to ask if Dyce's buck had been chewed up by foxes. Turns out the deer was in perfect condition. I could only suspect that Dyce had made up the story to save face. Funny how some people can't stop lying, even to themselves.

Hunting pressure on the first day of doe season was always heavy. And this day was no exception. Back then, Pennsylvania had but a two day antlerless season, which always ran on a Monday and Tuesday. It was the last chance for tens of thousands of hunters to kill a deer, and for many it was panic time. As a result, game wardens were kept busy chasing down one violation after another.

I hadn't gone more than a mile when I rounded a bend on a back road just as a pickup truck loaded with orange-clad hunters discharged two men from its bed. Leaping to the ground from each side, they stood stiffly and faced me, one at each corner of the bumper as I pulled behind the truck and parked. The others sat in the bed and watched with stunned faces when I exited my patrol car.

As I moved forward, the two human pillars sidestepped from their respective corners to block the tailgate like doormen at some posh nightclub. It didn't take a body-language expert to see that something was wrong here.

Suddenly a voice boomed from the back of the truck: "WHERE'S ALL THE DEER?" A large man with a great black beard came forward, the truck's bed creaking on its springs with each step. "We've been hunting all day and haven't seen a thing!"

He said this as if it were all my fault. I suspected he was trying to intimidate me. Hoping I'd stay back. I faced the two bodyguards at the tailgate and ordered them to step aside.

They looked at me with hardened faces, refusing to budge.

"Move or go to jail," I said. "Your choice."

The men exchanged nervous glances and looked up at the bearded man standing in the bed of the truck.

"He's a police officer, you fools! Do what he says."

They recoiled at his command and quickly moved aside, obviously fearing the man much more than they did me. I looked into the bed. A doe lay dead, surrounded by the five hunters sitting in a circle around it.

I said. "Who's the lucky hunter?"

No one answered.

I looked up at the bearded man, the only one standing in the truck. "Simple question, yet nobody wants to say!"

I reached behind the tailgate, pulled back on the center latch, and lowered it. The deer was lying just inside the bed with a bullet hole in its right ribcage. I grabbed a leg and pulled the carcass close so I could inspect the tag attached to its ear. It had been filled out completely, the hunter's name printed in pencil on its face.

"Which one of you is Ted Lansky?" I asked, looking up.

"He's not here," said the bearded man. "He had to leave for work."

I didn't believe him, and thought one of the men in the truck probably shot the deer and put Ted Lansky's tag on it so he could kill another one.

"How long ago did he leave?" I asked the bearded man.

"A while ago. He's probably halfway home by now."

"Where is home?"

"South Philly, why?"

"Step down from the truck," I said. "I want to see your license."

He frowned. "You want to see *my* license. Why?"

"If it'll make you feel better, I want to see everyone's license. I'm just starting with yours. Now get down off the truck."

He squatted heavily, and then sat on the tailgate. Shifting forward, he eased his considerable frame off the truck and turned around so I could take his license from the plastic holder pinned on the back of his orange vest. I opened it and read the name inside.

"I see you're a Lansky, too. Are you related to Ted?"

"He's my son."

"Does he live with you?"

"Yeah, he lives with me."

I looked at the five hunters seated in the truck's bed and focused on the one with frightened eyes, knees pulled protectively to his chest. "Was Ted Lansky hunting with you today?"

He nodded, his eyes shifting nervously to the bearded man then back to me.

The hunter next to him spoke up. "Ted shot the deer, officer," he said. "I helped him gut it and drag it back to the truck. Honest!"

I looked at the bearded man. "Is the phone number on your license still good?"

"Yeah. But if you're thinking about calling my son, you're wasting your time. He won't be home yet."

Even though there were no cell phones in those days, we still had our ways. I got back into my patrol vehicle, keeping a cautious eye on the hunters, and radioed headquarters. A dispatcher answered. I told him what was going on and gave him the phone number, requesting that he call and see if Ted Lansky picked up. With luck, we'd catch him home. If so, there were some questions I wanted the dispatcher to ask him.

Within minutes, the dispatcher radioed back. "I have Mr. Lansky on the phone with me right now. He says he was hunting this morning and killed a deer. I told him you have a few questions for him."

I keyed the mike. "Ask him what time he killed the deer."

"Stand by," he said. In a moment, he came back: "Says it was in the morning."

I checked my watch; it was past noon. Had it been killed in the morning, rigor mortis would have started. This deer was a fresh kill, still warm and pliable. On top of that, the TIME OF KILL section of the tag had PM checked off, not AM.

"Ten-four," I replied. "Ask him where he hit the deer."

He did equally miserable on his second answer, telling the dispatcher that he shot the deer just behind the left shoulder, when the bullet had struck the doe in the right side, and in the ribcage, not the shoulder. Finally, Ted Lansky struck out completely with his third answer. He claimed he had killed the deer on his grandmother's property in Blue Bell, but here we all were: his dad, the deer, his hunting buddies and the game warden, twenty miles north, in Skippack.

I hung up my mike and stepped out of the vehicle. The bearded man's eyes dropped when I looked at him. I had purposely lowered my side window while on the radio so he could overhear everything. He'd been listening to the dispatcher relay his son's answers and knew the game was over. Humiliated and ashamed, he admitted shooting the deer

139

and to using his son's tag. To make matters worse, he was transporting the deer in a vehicle with his hunting companions, making each of them an accomplice, and hence, liable for a two-hundred dollar fine apiece. And since they had all been so uncooperative, I had no problem arresting them. His son had become an accessory as well, by interfering with my investigation with his lies.

I confiscated the deer and secured it to my big game carrier. Then I collected everyone's hunting licenses, got back inside my car, and began copying down names, addresses, and other information I needed to prosecute them. The poachers gathered close, occasionally glancing my way as they exchanged nervous whisperings.

When I finished writing, I stepped back out and faced them, explaining their options of settling via field acknowledgments or taking court hearings, stating that citations would be forthcoming to anyone who didn't show up at the state police barracks on the following Saturday.

All remained silent, including the boisterous bearded man who had brought so much trouble their way.

I had nothing more to say to them. Breakfast had been years ago, it seemed. I needed to refuel, so I climbed back into my patrol car and made my way toward Speck's Drive-In near Collegeville for lunch.

Halfway through a plate of chicken and fries, I looked up to see Bob McConnell walk in the door. Although Bob was a deputy for the Fish and Boat Commission, we often patrolled together, and I waved him over to my table. He pulled out a chair and sat across from me. "Knew I'd find you here eventually. Been checking every half hour since noon."

"Why didn't you just call on the radio?"

"Mine quit on me this morning. How 'bout I hook up with you for the rest of the day."

I always enjoyed Bob's company and was glad he found me. "Sounds good. Lots going on today; I could use some help."

"Don't know how you've managed so far without me," he said with a smile in his eye.

"Have lunch yet? Might not get dinner."

"It's two o'clock, Bill. Lunch was hours ago. I'll just grab a cup of tea—sit here and watch you eat."

I stuffed a forkful of fries into my mouth and mumbled, "Suit yourself."

I couldn't help but notice a man sitting at the far counter staring at us. When McConnell walked by to get his tea, he called him over. I heard the man say something about a deer being shot. McConnell listened for a moment, then nodded his head my way, suggesting he talk to me directly about it.

As he started over, I couldn't help but wonder if he would have reported the violation had he not seen us here. Most likely not, I supposed. I couldn't count the number of times I'd stumbled upon someone with information about poaching who'd approached me only because we happened to cross paths.

He was in his early twenties with an unruly mop of red hair and a face full of freckles. "I don't mean to interrupt your lunch," he said, "but deer season isn't open or anything like that, is it?"

"Doe season is open," I said. "Why?"

He pulled out a chair and sat across from me, leaning forward as if to convey something in grand confidence. "My neighbor shot a deer this morning," he said in a low voice. "I think it was a buck. I was in my bedroom when I heard the shot, and when I looked outside I saw him running across the lawn in his long johns with a rifle in his hand. I watched him drag the carcass into his barn."

McConnell joined us, a Styrofoam cup in his hand. He grabbed a chair and sat. "Buck season is closed," he said, taking a sip of his tea. "Sure you saw antlers?"

"Yeah. It was a long way off, but I'm pretty sure about it." He frowned suddenly. "Look, I know this guy pretty well. Don't tell him I said anything, okay?"

"We'll leave you out of this," I assured him. "But we need more information before we can do anything. What's his name?"

He straightened in his chair and studied us painfully, as if he'd suddenly thought better of it, and I wondered if he was going to clam up.

McConnell suspected the same thing. "Did your neighbor see you this morning?" he asked.

"No way. He couldn't have."

"Then why would he suspect you?"

The young man regarded McConnell in contemplative silence.

"He'll never know you spoke to us," I told him. "You have my word on it."

I watched his eyes flick to McConnell and back to me, his shoulders slowly lowering into a posture of submission. "He's not somebody you want mad at you," he said. "His name is Mike Columbo. A rough guy with a bad temper. He's always shooting stuff: little birds, squirrels, rabbits. He picks up the carcasses and takes them into his barn. I guess he skins them in there and then brings them into his house and eats them." He wrinkled his nose and shuddered. "Poor little critters. Makes me sick."

I asked him where the deer was killed on the property, what time it was shot, how many people lived in the house, and what guns Columbo might have, then thanked him for the information and went to the counter for a takeout box. I still had almost half a chicken on my plate along with some fries, so I scooped everything into the container and started out the door with McConnell.

It was only a fifteen-minute drive to Columbo's place. He had ten acres on a seldom-used township road a mile from the county line. His house, a small cape cod with a stone front, sat at the end of a macadam driveway just off the road. The bulk of his property lay behind the house. Half was wooded, the remainder mowed lawn with a dozen apple trees scattered about. The fruit trees would attract deer, and I wondered how many he might have killed over the years.

142

Nestled halfway between the woods and Columbo's house was a large rectangular barn of unpainted vertical boards. It had an attractive A-frame roof and hinged wagon doors.

"Barn's closed," said McConnell. "Might need a search warrant."

"Hope not," I said. "We could spend the rest of the day doing the paperwork if we do."

I pulled into the driveway and parked, wondering whether anyone would come to the door once they looked out the window and saw two uniformed game wardens walking across the property. As we neared the front porch, we could hear loud voices talking excitedly inside.

"They know we're here," said McConnell.

I knocked and heard the frenzied thrashing of feet coupled with the sound of furniture being moved. Something large, like a pot, crashed to the floor. "State Game Commission!" I called through the door.

As quickly as the clamor began, it suddenly ceased. There was an extended moment of complete silence, then two muffled voices could be heard: one the utterance of a frantic woman, the other gruff and abrupt, obviously male. Heavy footsteps approached from the back of the house, and when the door swung wide open, a muscular man in his fifties stood there. He had a large balding head and a face blackened with stubble. He was dressed in blue jeans and a T-shirt, a thick shock of chest hair protruding from its V-neck opening.

"We're state conservation officers," I said. "We want to talk to you about the deer you shot this morning."

He looked at us like with feigned surprise. "What makes you think I shot a deer?"

I said, "Someone saw you, Mr. Columbo. It was a buck."

He frowned and shook his head. "Then someone must be lying, because I didn't shoot anything."

McConnell said, "Then why do you have blood stains on your shoes and pant legs?"

Columbo looked down. My eyes followed his. The stains, tiny spots, were just a few, and barely noticeable on his dark jeans and black shoes.

"You can invite us in or we'll get a search warrant," I said. "It's up to you."

He looked back into the house for a moment. Then, his voice low, he said, "Look, you're making my wife nervous. She's got a bad heart. I think you better leave. Like I told you, I got no deer in here."

I said, "Mr. Columbo, if you don't let us in, my deputy will stay here while I go into town and get a search warrant. When I come back, I'll have more uniformed officers with me, and we will search your house, your barn, your outbuildings and your vehicles. If you don't want that to happen, then I suggest you cooperate by telling the truth and allowing Officer McConnell and me to come inside."

He hung his head and nodded slowly. "That would really upset my wife. I guess I got no choice." He stepped back and motioned us forward. "C'mon, let's get this over with. Deer's in the kitchen."

The front door led directly into a spacious living room with a stone chimney that ascended to the ceiling. A log fire crackled in the fireplace, warming us immediately as we stepped inside. An oversized, plush leather couch faced the television. Eagles vs. Steelers. Too bad we couldn't watch. We followed Columbo straight back into the kitchen where we saw deer parts scattered everywhere. A huge pile of venison, cut and wrapped in white freezer paper, was stacked on the kitchen table, each package carefully marked for steaks, ground meat, chops, and roast.

The gray tile floor was spattered with gore, the kitchen sink covered in thick gobs of dried blood. A sloppy heap of deer lungs dangled over the counter by the sink, while a solitary pot of venison chunks boiled furiously upon the stove. Dumped in a corner to my right, lay a rumpled bag filled with fresh deer bones and fat.

Columbo's wife stood next to the stove wearing a blue wool sweater and a pink apron over baggy polyester slacks.

She stared at us wide-eyed, slowly backing away until she felt the counter pressing at her buttocks. She turned to her husband. "Why did you let these men in here, Michael? This is our home!"

Columbo raised his palms in a gesture of humility. "I got no choice, honey. They're game wardens. It's about the deer. I think I'm in trouble."

She looked at him, her face lined with worry. "Trouble? Why? It was killed on our land. That deer belonged to us."

I said, "Ma'am, that's not how it works. It's doe season. Your husband shot a buck, which makes it an unlawful kill."

"Whoa!" protested Columbo. "I never said I shot the deer. Somebody did, but it wasn't me. I was up in the bathroom when I heard a shot. When I looked out the window, I saw a buck come staggering out of the woods. It dropped dead right in my back yard, so I waited for them to come get it." He glanced at his wife then back to me. "Not that I would've let them keep it. I just wanted to catch the no good creep trespassing on my land." He shrugged dismissively. "When nobody showed up, I went out and claimed the deer for myself. I didn't think I did anything wrong."

My freckle-faced informant had told me he'd seen Columbo running toward the deer with a rifle in his hand after hearing a shot. If Columbo needed to save face by telling me someone else killed the deer, it was fine with me. But I was certain that wasn't the case.

"You should've called and reported it rather than keep it for yourself."

"But I didn't kill it," insisted Columbo. "And it would only have gone to waste!"

I said, "It would have been donated to a needy family, which is what's going to happen anyway because I'm confiscating it. You're in possession of an unlawfully killed deer. You can't keep it."

He shook his head and scowled. "So now what? I pay a fine or something?"

"That's right."

He glanced uneasily at his wife. "How much?"

"Three hundred dollars."

Columbo's wife let out a low groan and clutched at her chest, her face turning ghost white. Columbo caught her just as she swooned, gently lowering her body until she was sitting on the blood-spattered floor, he propped her back against a row of cabinets. She sat breathing in shallow, rapid gasps, mumbling something about her heart.

Columbo reached forward and yanked open a drawer full of medicine. He grabbed a small bottle and twisted open the lid, shaking a tiny pill into his palm. Then, as he gently placed it on his wife's lips, she touched his wrist tenderly and swallowed the tablet.

Columbo looked up and glared at us. "See what you've done to my wife!"

In typical outlaw form, he elected to blame us for the consequences of his dishonest act. I let it pass. "Want me to call for an ambulance?"

He shook his head. "She'll be okay. Just give her a few minutes." Kneeling by her side, he encouraged her in a low voice to stay calm, telling her everything would be all right. Soon her color began to return and she offered him a faint smile.

There was no need to stay any longer; our presence would only add to his wife's distress, so Deputy McConnell and I gathered the wrapped packages of illegal venison and took them out to my patrol car. As we were placing the confiscated meat into the back, Columbo walked out to meet us.

"The head and hide are in the barn," he said. "Guess you want that too."

I put the last package of venison inside and closed the door. "Why don't you show us."

We trailed him across the back yard. Along the way, Columbo pointed to where the deer dropped in his yard, the grass matted with dry blood. He opened the barn doors and stepped back. The hide was spread out on the floor, skin side up to dry. The head of a four-point buck lay next to it. I stepped inside and retrieved both. McConnell stood just outside the door with Columbo; they were looking at the back of his house as I walked outside.

"Nice place," offered McConnell.

"Thanks," said Columbo.

"Three bedrooms upstairs, huh."

Columbo glanced at him and then looked back at his house. "Master plus two small bedrooms. How'd you know?"

"You can tell by the size of the windows."

"You're a perceptive man," said Columbo.

McConnell nodded. "Jack and Jill bath between the two small bedrooms?"

Columbo looked surprised. "Yes, but there's no bathroom window to tell you this time. So how?—"

"Just a guess," McConnell said. "But the master has a bathroom window, correct?"

"That's right."

"And that window is on the side of your house. Right?"

"Correct again!"

"Which makes it impossible for you to have seen a deer staggering across your back yard from the bathroom window like you told us."

Columbo shook his head wearily. "Like I said, you're a perceptive man, officer. You're right. I lied to you. I was making breakfast this morning when I spotted the deer out the kitchen window. I opened the back door and shot it. Satisfied? You can send me a ticket in the mail and I'll pay the fine. Just please, take the deer and leave. I need to tend to my wife."

With that, he turned and walked toward his house. We left him go. McConnell and I had everything we needed to settle the case. We put the head and hide in my vehicle and continued patrolling the county until well after dark, apprehending several additional hunters with unlawfully killed deer. It was a busy first day, as all season openers were back then, and tomorrow would be even more hectic as the season would come to a close for tens of thousands of hunters who still hadn't killed their deer.

# Outlaw Trappers

**O**F ALL THE POACHERS I'VE DEALT WITH over the years, outlaw trappers have always been the most difficult. Even honest, law-abiding trappers are secretive by nature, often operating in the wee hours of the morning, under the cover of darkness, as they race to check their traps before clocking in with their regular jobs.

Trappers take great pains to hide traps set on land by covering them with loose soil or ground duff, their water sets are camouflaged as well. This is done not only to keep them hidden from the animals they target but to prevent people from discovering them as well. Steel traps are expensive and subject to thievery if not properly concealed. Once discovered, a thief can steal the traps as well as the valuable furbearers they hold, causing a tremendous loss to the hardworking trapper.

Most water trappers operate by vehicle, driving the back roads from one bridge crossing to another, checking their mink, muskrat or beaver traps right from the edge of the road. If the trap is empty, they jump back in the vehicle and head for the next set, leaving virtually no sign of their presence. And even when an animal is caught, they're careful not to leave any indication of human presence, approaching their traps by wading through the water so as not to leave boot prints in the muddy stream bank. Traps are often rigged to a slide wire with a one-way locking device so the captured animal drowns, thus remaining under the murky waters for no one to see.

Land trappers are even more difficult to detect. Often, their traps are set on private property—farms or large estates where they are free from exposure to outsiders. These too are often auto trappers, checking their sets from the comfort of pickup trucks, exiting only if a catch is made, where they quickly dispatch the animal and remake the set. They move fast, from one location to the next, as time is money to the trapper.

Unlike the typical big game hunter who often hunts with others and spends considerable time in a relatively small area waiting for a deer or bear to come by, the trapper is a loner who hustles from one location to another in an effort to tend as many traps as possible, making it difficult for a game warden to catch up to them.

There aren't all that many trappers operating these days, and, in fact, with the exception of the occasional fur boom when prices skyrocket, they've always been few in numbers, especially when compared to the number of hunters in any given area. And due to their secretive nature, most people never know a trapper is operating in their area unless they happen to blunder into an animal caught in one of their traps.

The odds of a game warden catching someone in the act of setting or checking traps are slim at best. Many of my cases against trappers were initiated by someone who called to report a trespassing violation. I also managed to make a few cases—very few, in fact, throughout my long career—by walking stream banks to check for illegally set traps; however, I found it to be extremely time consuming and largely unproductive.

But just because a game warden manages to find an illegal trap or catch up with a trapper who is operating unlawfully, doesn't mean he'll be able to make an arrest. Outlaw trappers are some of the most difficult people to prosecute in court. The art of trapping is a mystery to most folks, including many game wardens. And unlike hunting, most judges, including those serving in rural areas, have virtually no understanding whatsoever about animal traps or trapping.

Another hurdle to their successful prosecution is that trappers are almost never caught in the act of setting traps, either legally or illegally. In almost every instance, cases against trappers are brought about after-the-fact, by discovering traps that have been set unlawfully. The trapper is nowhere to be found at the time, for he is someplace else, checking other traps, which can number in the hundreds in some instances.

The most serious trapping violations are traps set in closed season and taking over the legal limit of furs. Either violation is considered outright poaching. But again, tracking down a trapper while he is in the act of setting traps is akin to catching a ghost on camera. However, because I have a background in fur trapping, I've been able to piece together a number of cold cases over the years. Unfortunately, unlike my prosecution record against unlawful hunters, which was highly successful, I lost many court cases against trappers due to a lack of familiarity with the sport by the judges hearing my cases. This was particularly frustrating to me because I ran a trapline every winter since early boyhood but still had great difficulty persuading the judges presiding over these cases to rule in my favor.

A good example would be a case I lost against a mink trapper toward the end of my career. Mink are ever-hungry predators that spend much of their time along waterways hunting for prey. Trappers know that mink hug bridge walls as they travel streams in search of something to kill. A well-known method for catching these sleek furbearers is to set a small-jawed foothold trap tight against a bridge wall so it will be positioned properly for any passing mink. The farther away from the wall, the more likely you are to catch a (much larger and wider legged) raccoon instead.

So one afternoon during raccoon season—the day prior to the mink opener—when I spotted a small trap commonly used for mink and muskrats set under an inch of water, flush against a bridge wall, it left no doubt about the trapper's intention. To make the case even more compelling, there was a virtual highway of mink tracks in the muddy stream-bottom alongside the wall, and the trap had been set directly on top of the tracks. A thin strand of wire had been used to attach the trap to a six-foot dead branch no thicker than an ax handle. Although this setup would keep the average two-pound mink from getting very far, it would never hold the typical ten to fifteen pound raccoon. Even the smallest of them would soon escape by running off with the branch dragging behind until it snagged on something, at which time the powerful raccoon would soon pull free.

The trap was tagged with the owner's name and address as required by law. It was an experienced trapper whom I'd suspected of poaching for many years. Apparently, he thought no one would find his trap, and since raccoon season was in, with mink season opening the following morning, he undoubtedly believed he'd be safe with anything he caught.

And he would have been, had I not discovered his trap.

When I filed a citation against him for trapping in closed season, he hired an attorney and requested a hearing with the local district justice. We went to trial, and I lost. The fact that the trap had been set on a virtual mink highway didn't mean anything to the judge, who only understood that a trap had been set during raccoon season, and the defendant claimed he intended to catch a raccoon, not a mink. That was good enough. The thing that really frustrated me was that the defendant and I were highly skilled trappers with decades of experience, and we both knew he was guilty. The only person who thought he was innocent was the judge.

Unfortunately, this was the way most of my trapping cases concluded. When I found traps set illegally with the owner's tag attached, the trapper would simply claim his trap had been stolen and that someone else must have made the illegal set. And because no one saw him setting the trap, he'd get away with it. Hence, my luck with outlaw trappers was dismal at best—with one grand exception. And it is a story that I'd like to share with you now.

His name was Zachariah Slugg, and the case dates all the way back to nineteen seventy-nine when Slugg was trapping on private property without permission and caught the landowner's German shepherd in one of his traps. Though the dog suffered little more than a tender paw, it prompted an immediate call to the Game Commission by the infuriated landowner.

Although game wardens did not enforce trespass laws in those days, I traveled out to Willow Grove to investigate the incident anyway, hoping to make a case. But the trap had been untagged, which left me with no leads as to who might have set it.

After speaking with the landowner and collecting the trap for evidence, I decided to walk over to a small stream at the back of his fifty-acre estate to see if I could find more traps. My intention was to pull up any I discovered so his dog wouldn't get tangled again.

As luck would have it, I happened to run into Zachariah Slugg as he was leaving the property with a handful of traps. His truck had been parked in an inconspicuous location along a narrow township road, and he was about to make his getaway when I called out to him.

"State Game Warden! Hold up!"

He turned and stood facing me, a thickset man of medium height with snow-white hair that fell to his shoulders. I was in full uniform and walked directly to him. "Let's see the traps," I said.

Slugg said nothing. Simply handed the traps over without a word. There were eight of them. All untagged. Checking further, I found that he didn't have a trapping license either, so I arrested him on the spot.

Slugg paid his fine the following week in cash. But only nine months later, he was caught trapping illegally once again. My deputy was investigating a complaint about a trapper operating too close to a residential neighborhood when he discovered a trap with a ten-inch jaw spread set atop a fallen tree in the woods. The trap was baited with fish, which would lure any number of animals, both wild and domestic. State law prohibits setting these devices outside of waterways because they are designed to capture and kill large furbearing animals like beavers by closing around their chest or neck; hence, they can easily kill small domestic pets.

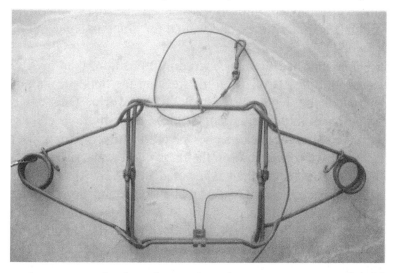

I was surprised to learn that the trap was tagged with Slugg's name and address, as required by law. Outlaw trappers commonly leave their traps untagged, making it more difficult to catch up to them. Slugg must have forgotten to remove the tag, which made my job so much easier. I simply called him on the phone and made arrangements to meet him at the state police barracks the following Saturday. He never bothered to make an excuse or argue with me about the fine. He showed up on time, brought cash, and settled on a field acknowledgement of guilt. It seemed the man just wanted to do things his own way, and if it meant paying an occasional fine, so be it. And so, I began to develop a nasty feeling about Slugg, thinking that my second run-in with the man would not be the last.

Two weeks later, my expectations were fulfilled when I received an anonymous tip claiming Slugg was working a trapline in a heavily populated section of Montgomery County. With every reason to suspect he might be trapping illegally, I assigned a deputy to the case, asking him to begin a systematic patrol of the area. Two days and a hundred miles of road-wear later, the deputy managed to locate

Slugg's truck parked along a township road adjacent to a large woodlot bordering a residential neighborhood. He quickly positioned himself farther up the road where he wouldn't be readily seen and waited for Slugg to come out of the woods.

No sooner had he maneuvered into position, than he saw Zachariah Slugg stroll from the trees on the opposite side of the road as if he hadn't a care in the world. Dressed in camouflage clothes, clutching a dozen traps by their chains, he looked straight ahead as he walked toward his truck. But just as he was about to drop the traps into the back, he froze. Then, as if someone had whispered in his ear that he was being watched, he slowly did an about-face and stood staring at the deputy's vehicle.

Once again, Slugg was caught red-handed. Although he had finally purchased a license, he kept it unlawfully concealed inside his coat so no one would suspect he was trapping. And when the deputy looked at his traps, he found that they were all untagged so they couldn't be traced back to him.

Later that week, Slugg met me at the state police barracks once again and paid his fines in cash for the untagged traps as well as for failure to display his license and for trapping in a safety zone (within one hundred and fifty yards of occupied buildings). Because this was his third apprehension in less than twelve months, the Game Commission revoked his hunting and trapping privileges for two years.

He fell completely off the radar after that; however, I suspected he was operating in a neighboring county, far from my patrol zone, so I alerted all game wardens in the surrounding counties to be on the lookout for him. Unfortunately, no one ever reported seeing any sign of Zachariah Slugg.

Four years later, just prior to trapping season, I received a phone call from a man who'd been angrily confronted by a grizzled old trapper in a pickup truck as he attempted to release a squirrel from a trap on his property. He was taken aback by the man's hostile attitude, especially considering that he'd never given him permission to be there. When the landowner refused to hand over the trap, the man shouted out an obscenity and stormed off in his pickup. Fortunately, the landowner thought to jot down the tag number on a notepad as he fled.

I wasn't surprised when I ran the plate and it came back to Zachariah Slugg. The trapper's disregard for private property, coupled with his belligerent stance toward the landowner, had fit him to a tee.

I drove out to meet with the landowner, and he took me to the location of the trap. It was a Victor number two, double coil spring, commonly used by fox trappers in those days. It had also been set in a manner frequently used to catch foxes, known as a dirthole set. The squirrel had simply blundered into it. After searching the property for additional traps, and finding none, I decided to get a search warrant for Zachariah Slugg's property.

Although trapping season wouldn't open for another week, it looked like Slugg was up to his old tricks again, and I suspected he would have some illegal furs stashed at his house. But in order to find them, I'd have to convince the local judge that my hunch had merit so he'd issue the warrant. Bearing in mind how cautious judges can be when it came to granting search warrants, my prospects seemed dismal at best, especially when I considered my track record with trappers I'd brought before the courts in past years.

Thinking I might need help, I made a telephone call to my neighboring officer in Bucks County, Ed Bond, and asked if he could assist me with the case. Bond, a well-respected veteran game warden and close friend, teamed up with me a short time later, and I briefed him on Slugg's history as we drove to the judge's chambers in Abington.

City born-and-raised, the judge knew nothing about trapping and little more about wildlife in general. But he was gracious enough to allow an audience with Bond and me. We sat in his private office for what seemed an eternity as I went over the details of my case against Slugg. He listened politely, his face portraying a subtle skepticism as I explained all about trap sizes and their jaw spreads and how each trap is designed by the manufacturer for a specific range of animals. I explained how trappers target certain animals by studying their habits and behavior patterns, and then go about setting traps in locations these animals are known to frequent. I talked about modern trapping techniques and sets, especially the dirthole set—by far, the most popular method used by fox trappers. I explained Zachariah Slugg's background as an outlaw trapper with multiple prosecutions, and I went into great detail about my personal background as a fox trapper. In the end, I was able to sway the judge in my favor, and he granted a search warrant for not only Slugg's house, but his outbuildings and his personal vehicle as well.

Later that morning, as Ed Bond and I drove toward Zachariah Slugg's house, I thought back to the first time I met Bond. Ironically, it was as a fourteen-year-old trapper when my father took me to see the game warden so I could present him with the dried pelt of a gray fox I'd caught. In those days, the Game Commission paid a four-dollar bounty on foxes provided the trapper brought the hide to a game warden, who would split the animal's nose with a pair of scissors and then type up a report to be filed in Harrisburg describing the details of its killing. Bond, a handsome man in his twenties, was dressed in a clean, well-creased khaki shirt with a glossy Game Protector badge pinned to his chest. His forest-green trousers had a black stripe running down the outside of each leg, his black boots polished to a gleaming smoothness. I was impressed. And although fifty years have passed since that day, I still remember it vividly.

Bond and I traveled only a few miles before I found myself turning a corner into Slugg's neighborhood, and I immediately began to worry that we may not find anything after serving the warrant. If I drew a blank with the search, I feared it could damage my credibility in future cases with the judge. Although Slugg was an accomplished trapper, who had taken his share of furs over the years, I was acting primarily on a hunch. Hence, I began to question myself: What if he hadn't caught anything in his traps so far—and even if he had, what if the furs had been stashed someplace other than his house? I'd have to return to the judge empty-handed. I'd feel like a fool. But as I ruminated over these unsettling prospects, I also realized it was too late to turn back. Zachariah Slugg's house loomed just ahead. And it was time to step up to the plate.

A typical suburban two-story bungalow, Slugg's house sat midway along a long row of similar homes built back in the fifties. I parked out on the road and walked to the front door with Bond. I was concerned that Slugg's pickup truck wasn't in the driveway as I'd hoped it would be, and I wondered if anyone would be home.

Although the search warrant allowed us to enter the premises even if empty, it wasn't something either of us wanted to do.

To my relief, when I pushed on the doorbell I heard footsteps approaching. When the door opened, a woman in her thirties stood before us with a dishtowel in her hands, looking puzzled by our uniforms. I informed her that Bond and I were state game wardens and showed her the search warrant, explaining that we were investigating a game law violation and that she would have to let us in to search the house. She nodded stiffly and backed away, her knuckles turning white against the dishtowel.

"This is about my father, isn't it?" she said anxiously. "He lives here with me."

"Yes, ma'am," I said. "We're looking for animal pelts he might be keeping here. Do you know of any?"

She shook her head and frowned. "I have no idea. The man comes and goes as he pleases. I try to stay out of his way."

"I understand," I said. "You're welcome to accompany us as we search."

She backed three steps to a sofa and plopped herself down, her head bowed, forearms settled on her lap. "No. I feel a little weak-kneed," she said softly. "I think I'll just sit here awhile."

"I'd like to start with the garage?"

She nodded. "There's a door in the kitchen that leads into it."

"Yes, ma'am. Sorry about this. Do you have an attic?"

She nodded politely and looked away. "Down the hall."

I walked past her into the kitchen and opened the door into the garage while Bond went up into the attic and looked around. As a trapper, I'd always kept my pelts hanging from a wooden beam in my garage so they'd dry properly. When I didn't find any furs in Slugg's garage, my confidence began to wane.

I stepped back into the house and waited for Bond, hoping to hear him holler down that he'd found something. But there were no furs in the attic, either, and I began to think the search warrant had been a mistake.

Only the basement remained, and when Bond and I walked down a long flight of wooden steps onto the cold cement floor, we were surprised to find the place empty with the exception of a large chest freezer sitting along a far wall. My vision of trapping equipment scattered about the basement floor and furs drying on wooden boards disappeared like water down a drain. A white metal chest, six feet long by four feet high, was all that stood between success and failure. All I needed was to find one carcass from Slugg's trapline inside. Fox, coon, muskrat—whatever. I didn't care. Trapping season was closed, so anything I found would be illegal.

The concrete floor seemed to stretch for a mile as Bond and I crossed to the freezer. The garage and attic had showed no signs of any trapping activity, and the basement was squeaky clean with nothing to indicate anyone had ever set foot down here. I couldn't help but think about the embarrassment I'd face if we had to return to the judge's chambers empty-handed.

When I reached the freezer, I envisioned it chocked full of frozen meats and vegetables from the local market, and my stomach tightened into a nauseating knot. I paused for a moment and glanced at my partner, then I unsnapped the latch and raised the lid.

There was a burst of red fur. My eyes became riveted to the inside chamber. A fox! Several of them! I reached down and began pulling frozen carcasses from the freezer: one fox, two, three, then four—followed by two large raccoons. A wave of relief washed over me, and I realized, as I always did when a poacher was caught, that this was the reason why I became a game warden.

Bond couldn't help but smile. "Good job, Bill!" said my partner. "You've got him cold, now."

I chuckled at the pun, but my humor was suddenly cut short when we heard the pounding of heavy footsteps on the kitchen floor above us. It was Zachariah Slugg. His harsh, booming voice rolled down the basement steps as he berated his daughter for letting us enter his home.

"What is wrong with you, girl?" he roared. "They can't just walk in here like this! They got no right!"

Bond and I had no idea what to expect next. Thinking he might become violent toward his daughter, we scrambled upstairs to confront him.

Slugg heard our boots hammering the wooden steps as we ascended. When we burst into the kitchen, he was waiting there, hands on his hips, cold gray eyes glaring defiantly. "What's going on here?" he demanded. "This is my home!"

We were in full uniform. My marked patrol car was parked right outside. There was no mistake who we were, but I declared our identity just the same. "State Game Commission! We have a search warrant."

Slugg's head jerked back, his face a mask of confusion and surprise. "You have what?"

I pulled the warrant from my back pocket and handed it to him. He took the folded paper, his hands trembling (rage or fear—I wasn't sure which) as he opened it.

"We looked in the freezer," I said. "We found the foxes and raccoons. Season's closed. But you already know that."

Slugg handed the warrant back to me, his jawline gradually softening with the grim realization that he'd been caught once again.

"Never should have stopped when I saw that guy messing with the squirrel in my trap," he grumbled. "Guess he reported me, huh?"

"You shouldn't have been on his property," I said.

Slugg pulled a chair from the kitchen table, waved an inviting hand for us to join him, and sat heavily. "Might as well get this over with," he said. "What's the fine this time?"

"We'll get to that later," I said as Bond and I took seats on each side of him.

Slugg's daughter was standing by the sink watching us with frightened eyes. Slugg looked over at her. "Sorry I yelled at you, sweetie."

She nodded in silence, then left the room, her footsteps trailing down the hallway. A door closed somewhere, a back bedroom I presumed. Then a hush fell over the house.

I was certain that Slugg had more traps set illegally somewhere, and that they would be untagged because it was closed season. But I hadn't the faintest notion where they might be. Although I'd had rotten luck prosecuting trappers in the past, I'd been batting a thousand with Zachariah Slugg ever since our first encounter, so I decided to use some trickery, hoping it might work in my favor.

Lacing my fingers together, I looked him in the eye and leaned forward, "How long have you been a trapper?"

"All my life."

"Me too." I said.

Slugg's stony gray eyes studied me for a while. Then he chuckled bitterly. "I'm not surprised. I can't seem to do anything without you sneaking up behind me."

I nodded. Then, as if I'd just looked into a crystal ball, I said, "I know you have fox and coon traps out right now."

Slugg frowned, his eyes searching my face.

I continued: "If I have to hunt every inch of the county until I find them—and I *will* find them—I'm going to charge you with a separate offense of trapping in closed season for every single trap." I paused for a moment to let the notion sink in.

"On the other hand," I added, "if you want to save me the time and trouble, and show me where they are, I'll only prosecute you for the furs in your freezer and a single closed season offense. I'll also let you off the hook on any untagged traps you have out."

Slugg thought about it for a moment. "Do I have your word on that?" he said.

"You have my word."

He slapped the table with two meaty hands. "Let's go!" He stood from his chair. "I'll take you to them right now."

I have to admit, I was more than surprised when he agreed. I can only assume he thought I had a fair idea about where he was trapping and figured I would eventually find them anyway. I'm sure he was also concerned about the likelihood of his trapping privileges being revoked again and hoped his cooperation might make a difference.

After retrieving the unlawfully caught animals from Slugg's freezer and securing them inside my patrol car, we followed Slugg's pickup truck toward his trapline. We tailed him for several miles until he turned into an abandoned farm and parked next to the charred remains of the house and barn that once occupied the place. As we followed him across a grassy field on foot, I noticed that he didn't have a license displayed on his back. I asked him about it.

Slugg, just ten feet ahead, stopped dead in his tracks. He turned slowly, the warm November sun glistening across the white stubble of his unshaven skin. "I don't have a license, my traps are untagged, and I don't have permission to trap here," he declared. "I'm a complete outlaw!"

With that, he turned abruptly and stomped across the field, cutting into a sparsely wooded area. Bond and I stayed close behind until Slugg stopped by a small stream and pointed out his first illegal set. A hole had been dug into the

161

bank and baited with a dead fish. A foothold trap lay under an inch of water in front of it, its jaws waiting for a hungry raccoon to investigate. Slugg bent down and yanked the trap from the water, along with it came an iron stake connected to its chain. As suspected, the trap was untagged.

We continued following Slugg along his illicit trapline, pulling one raccoon set after another until we ended up with fifteen traps, all of them untagged.

"That's it," he said. "You got them all."

"No fox traps?" I said.

"Nope!"

I doubted it. Locating traps set along a narrow stream for raccoons is an easy task. Just follow the waterway and they'll practically jump out at you. But finding fox traps camouflaged with ground cover and scattered over a hundred-acre field would be an entirely different matter, and Slugg knew it. The sun would soon set, making it almost impossible to find them, so I decided to settle with what we had for the day.

Back at my patrol car, I took a citation box from the seat and wrote citations for trapping in closed season and for the unlawful possession of the six animals in his freezer. As promised, I left him off the hook for the untagged traps. Still, his fines totaled almost nine hundred dollars.

He looked over the citations and stuffed them in his pocket without so much as a whimper, seemingly satisfied with it all.

Later that week, Slugg pled guilty before a district judge, and, as always, paid his fine with cash.

The following week, as I cruised by the same abandoned farm where Slugg had been setting traps for out-of-season raccoons, I noticed his pickup truck parked in plain view by the edge of a wooded area, and although trapping season was officially open, I felt compelled to check him when he returned to his vehicle. I had yet to meet Zachariah Slugg when he wasn't breaking the law, and wondered if perhaps this might be the day.

After waiting for a half hour or so, Slugg came walking out of the woods with a tangle of traps in his hand. He spotted me from a distance and stopped, abruptly turning his back to display the hunting license pinned to his coat. I suppose he thought I might wave a friendly hand of acknowledgement and be on my way when I saw he was "legal." But, of course, that would have been absurd considering his past. So, as he ambled toward his truck, refusing all the while to glance my way, I walked directly over to meet with him.

"How's the trapping today?" I inquired.

He tossed the traps into the bed of the truck and walked over to the cab. "Been better," he grumbled, opening the driver's door. He started to get in, when I spotted a twenty-two Remington rifle laying on the seat.

"Is that loaded?" I asked.

"Of course it is!" he scoffed. "What good's an empty gun?" Slugg seemed genuinely bewildered by my question, as though I'd asked if his tires had air in them.

"It's illegal to have a loaded gun in your vehicle—that is, unless you have a concealed weapons permit. Do you?"

"I got a hunting license. Ain't that enough?"

I moved past him and reached inside the cab to retrieve his gun. After removing a fully loaded magazine, I pulled the bolt back ejecting a round from the chamber. It seemed that the man was born to lose. And I couldn't help but wonder if he had some kind of learning disorder.

"You get a free Game Law Digest with your hunting license," I said as I thumbed the bullets from his magazine into my palm and dumped them into my coat pocket. "You really ought to start reading it."

"You're not gonna fine me for having bullets in my rifle, are ya?"

"How about the traps?" I said, ignoring the question. "Got 'em tagged this time?"

Slugg stared back at me. Then he hung his head and sighed. "Nope. They ain't tagged at all. Not one." He nodded at the traps in the truck's bed. "Had them set for coon, but I still got a few fox sets out."

"You know the routine," I said. "Let's go yank them up."

Once again, I found myself following Zachariah Slugg along his trapline. After finding three traps set for fox, each untagged, I escorted him back to my vehicle and had him stand there while I opened a citation pad and begin writing tickets for the loaded gun and the illegal traps. Slugg watched me for a while without saying a word, but his expression grew darker by the second, and I sensed a rage brewing inside him.

Suddenly, he launched into a furious tirade, accusing me of purposely singling him out and harassing him. He howled about how I wouldn't leave him alone, his face turning beat red. His chest heaved. Spittle flew from his lips. The veins in his neck swelled like eels. He tore off his coat and ripped his license from the plastic holder. Swearing he would never set another trap again, he began tearing the cardboard license into tiny pieces. But when he was about to slam them to the ground, I quickly warned him not to:

"Do it and I'll add a littering charge to your list of violations."

He froze with his arm raised, fist clutching the shredded license. Realizing I was dead serious, he dropped his arm and stuffed the pieces into his coat pocket. Then he stood and watched in rigid silence as I finished writing his tickets.

I wrote two citations: one for his untagged traps and another for the loaded firearm. As a result, Slugg was in debt to the Game Commission for another three hundred dollars plus court costs. I handed him the paperwork and got into my patrol car. And as I drove off, I couldn't quite bring myself to believe that Zachariah Slugg was through with trapping as he had sworn.

Several months later, Slugg received official notice from Harrisburg that his hunting and trapping privileges would be revoked for three years, and it looked like his vow to quit trapping was appropriate after all. But the lack of a license had never stopped him from trapping in the past; so, when I began to hear grumblings that he was running a trapline in the southern part of my district the following winter, I wasn't a bit surprised.

Determined to apprehend the outlaw, my deputies and I beefed up patrols in the area and eventually caught him checking traps along a stream down by the Philadelphia line. Once again, his traps were untagged, and many had been set in safety zones.

A subsequent lengthy investigation revealed that he'd been trapping for fifty days while under revocation before we managed to catch up to him. We also learned that he had been selling his unlawfully caught furs under a fictitious name to unsuspecting fur buyers in the area. Because he may have used several aliases, we were uncertain how many pelts were actually sold, or to whom, but managed to come up with six raccoons, two foxes, and three opossums that had been sold illegally to one particular buyer.

Once again, Zachariah Slugg pled guilty to all charges filed against him and paid his fine in cash—a whopping twenty-four hundred dollars, which was an unprecedented sum for a poacher to pay in those days.

For more than a decade after that, no one—neither I, my deputies, nor any neighboring wardens from other counties—ever saw or heard of Zachariah Slugg again. And I began to wonder if he'd simply vanished off the face of the earth.

Then, many years later, my partner Ed Bond reported that he'd seen him. He and his wife were at a Philadelphia nightclub when to their great surprise they saw Zachariah Slugg with a tall, attractive woman. They were dancing in long continuous movements across the ballroom floor. The music was big band, which suited them perfectly claimed my partner, for they were dancing to rhythm of the foxtrot.

# About the Author

William Wasserman, a third-degree black belt in Korean karate and a former national bodybuilding champion, has written seven books about his life as a state game warden. He received numerous awards for his work in wildlife conservation, including the United Bowhunters of Pennsylvania Game Protector of the Year Award, Pennsylvania Game Commission Northeast Region Outstanding Wildlife Conservation Officer, National Society Daughters of the American Revolution Conservation Medal, and the Pennsylvania Trappers Association Presidential Award. Wasserman has been published in several national magazines including Black Belt, Pennsylvania Game News, Fur-Fish-Game, South Carolina Wildlife, International Game Warden, and The Alberta Game Warden. Wasserman retired from the Pennsylvania Game Commission after thirty-two years of dedicated service and lives in South Carolina with his wife, Maryann.